Sean Patrick Guthrie

The Purple Dog Path to the U.S. Senate 2016

Sean Patrick Guthrie

DEDICATION

For Mom, Dad, Tricia, Barbara, Derek, Ronald, extended family, my friends, and especially to all the challengers of the status quo.

CONTENTS

ACKNOWLEDGMENTS

A heartfelt "Thank You" goes out to all of those who helped or advised in any way. If I listed everyone, this book would be at least double its current size. Always remember that we can create positive change together.

Sean Patrick Guthrie

1   A BRIEF BACKGROUND

Purpose of this Book

Greetings! The intent of *The Purple Dog Path to the U.S. Senate 2016* is to provide a fairly broad outline of my views while introducing myself to you.

First, you will be glad to know I am not a politician! I am just one common and regular citizen out of many eclectic and assorted Floridians. I am a candidate for this office trying to do my part in aiding the growing effort to steer us away from disaster and to bring civil service back to government. Politics as usual may be holding us hostage and dragging us away from real prosperity, but as an independent candidate not running under a party banner, I can represent Florida and America as we make real and tangible progress throughout the 21st century. I am definitely not your typical breed.

I often do things in a different manner than most, take the path less taken, and am definitely not afraid of being contrarian. The story I have been told goes that I crawled backwards most of the time as a baby, but when I started walking I never even once went back to crawling. Never blindly accepting the status quo or simply abiding by the conventional way of doing things must be in my DNA. I am a firm believer that we should question everything while being open to change in light of new evidence.

I like to joke that at the most basic level, we are all just idiots. Doubt it? Just look at how badly we can collectively treat each other. Jokes are often based in truth and when you think about it, we truly are just an advanced species of idiot animals doing idiot things while living on an average-sized planet in an average section of an average galaxy yet we act like we are the center of life, the universe, and everything.

Even though we are insignificant at the cosmic level, we can of course make large and life-changing impacts on our fellow human beings and even on the rest of the planet. To me, it underscores our responsibility to deal more kindly with one another because there is no hint that help is going to come from elsewhere to save us from ourselves. Taking old beliefs down from ideological pedestals and reexamining them in the light of the 21st century is long overdue in many cases.

Equality of opportunity is one such area which we must reexamine: our systems are failing common Floridians and Americans. With inequality so rampant, I wish to encourage others to not only passively support the effort for true equality, but to actively seek level playing fields by becoming involved in the political process. This is just as important as voting because democracy must always be safeguarded and we can always use fresh ideas in government.

Do not feel as though you have to sell out or must work your way up a political party's food chain. Independent candidates can compete and spread information via a variety of means and must fight against big money and its long political reach. In this day and age, every reason exists to be informed about candidates as access to information is at an all-time high. Making use of the availability and variety of media will help non-partisan candidates avoid typical campaign expenses as well. Keeping costs low and manageable is necessary as any movement needs participation at all levels.

My other current book, *The Purple Dog Path to the U.S. Senate 2016 Companion Book: It Takes a Village idiot*, is meant to be a humorous look at politics and government because the last thing I want to come across as is holier-than-thou. At the end of the day I'm just one person with what I feel are good ideas for improving our situation and I can offer nonpartisan, not bought or paid for, common sense leadership that we need instead of having to go through yet another cycle of the same politicians conducting partisan politics as usual.

You will see the many ways in which I am completely

different from career politicians and from politicians in general. If fortunate enough to represent the people of Florida and defend our Constitution, I would plan on seeking only a single reelection, therefore serving two terms at most. I believe that is adequate time to make a positive impact and to operate within the institution without becoming institutionalized. That, of course, is putting the cart way before the horse, but I wish to impress upon you I am not a political insider and that I am simply a citizen trying to make a positive difference and restore leadership to our gridlocked governmental system.

Many would say I am a Progressive candidate influenced by former Secretary of Labor Robert B. Reich, Senator Elizabeth Warren, and Senator Bernie Sanders. I am a candidate proposing a "Middle-Out" economic approach to finally re-strengthen the middle class and allow national prosperity. Simply put, I believe we can get the work done that politicians always talk about doing by not leaving it to the true politicians.

Assorted Facts About Me

- Born in Ohio at Wright-Patterson Air Force Base and have lived in Florida for over 32 years

- Grew up in the Florida panhandle in Niceville (located next to Eglin Air Force Base)

- Graduated with honors from Florida State University with a degree in Risk Management and Insurance, attended FSU's MBA program and Stetson University College of Law

- Worked in business for many years from adjusting insurance claims to financial advising and also as a financial controller and risk manager

- Owner and CEO of Purple Dog Enterprises, which is comprised of four small businesses:
    o Purple Dog Animal Sanctuary (non-profit)
    o Purple Dog Business Consulting, Inc.
    o Purple Dog Financial, Inc. (ceased operations because the financial industry makes me want to vomit)
    o Purple Dog Leadership, Inc.

- Longtime Habitat for Humanity volunteer

- Both my hips have been replaced because of avascular necrosis (airport security is no fun)

- I perform stand up often and love to write many types of comedy

- Other passions include science, math, and learning about astronomy and particle physics

Why the Name "Purple Dog?"

"You're either a Purple Cow or you aren't. You're either
remarkable, or you're invisible. Make your choice."
– Seth Godin

*Purple Cow: Transform Your Business by Being
Remarkable,* written by renowned entrepreneur, public
speaker, and worldwide bestselling author Seth Godin,
looks at how to differentiate yourself from a crowded
field of competitors. He begins the book with a story of
his family's drive through France. Hundreds of cows
lined the picturesque and beautiful landscape for
kilometers on end, but within twenty minutes the
Godins didn't even notice the cows. New ones down
the road were just like the old ones. Cows had become
worse than common... they were boring.

But what if the landscape happened to be dotted with
a purple cow amongst the regular, nondescript, boring
cows? Now that would be remarkable! That would be
something you would tell your friends about! That
would be interesting!

Godin says in order to compete in the 21st century you
must be remarkable and rise above the sea of cookie-
cutter clones and paint-by-number methodologies to
become like that purple cow. Purple cows like Apple,
Starbucks, Netflix, and HBO all dispense with
conventional thinking while operating against the status
quo and have benefitted because of it.

Additionally, combining the colors red and blue results in purple. Purple is an excellent symbol of unity because both political parties need to get their acts together and operate for the benefit of all the people and not the select few on either side.

My 501 (c) (3) non-profit is Purple Dog Animal Sanctuary and its initial focus is helping abandoned senior dogs. I have been around countless dogs and other animals my entire life and wish to give something back because they have enriched my life tremendously. Sanctuary expansion will be done in stages to allow care for other species of animals as well. Being fresh, unique, different, and an animal lover, the brand name Purple Dog was a no-brainer.

I will be providing you with much more personal information along the way, but for now let us start by taking a glimpse of our current political system before diving into specific issues.

Rage Against the Political Machine

Do we, the people, have any power or ability to change the system? Who is in control anyway?

American corporations currently exert far more political influence than their counterparts in other countries. Just look at the total mess that influence has created. Small businesses and their owners are being gouged as they do the work and pay the taxes that the largest corporations avoid. It would be one thing if enormous corporations backed off once it became evident that they were a leading driver of income inequality, however they press on instead and average citizens may be talking, but lawmakers certainly aren't listening.

Professors Martin Gilens of Princeton and Benjamin Page of Northwestern University analyzed 1,799 policy issues and found that "the preferences of the average American appear to have only a miniscule, near-zero, statistically non-significant impact upon public policy." As of now, regular people have no influence. We need to change that.

Lawmakers constantly follow the money and bend to the demands of the ultra-wealthy and Wall Street. Those entities and their lobbyists have no allegiance to our country. Their interests are totally misaligned with the interests of the people and it is demonstrated when those same huge companies threaten to leave every year as part of their tax complaint platform. Not only have they been doing it for years, but they are still more than ready to sell us out to make a buck because their only allegiance is to shareholders. Why else would they shift their wealth to foreign countries to avoid paying their fair share back to the very American people who buy their products, use their services, and help them stay in business in the first place?

Governments in other nations often bind corporate interests to those of workers and organized labor through legislation. American corporations distribute a smaller share to their workers than European or Canadian companies and American executives make substantially more than those in other wealthy countries. Nationwide, our CEOs' pay is exploding and big business is currently experiencing the biggest profit margins in 40 years all while the rank and file workers in the U.S. receive stagnant wages, work longer hours, receive less vacation time, and are not even guaranteed maternity leave.

Republicans and Democrats in power are absolutely horrible. Their so-called "leadership" has led not only to a stagnant middle class and poor, but their abject ineptitude continues to show little indication of providing true help in the future. Just like corporations with misaligned interests, both major parties are not aligned with the needs of the people, and neither Democrats nor Republicans do what they say they will. In the end, it's always the big money that gets their ear.

Elite Democrats are currently proving they are on par with Republicans when it comes to shady dealings. President Obama is currently pressing for approval of the secretive Trans Pacific Partnership (TPP) without debate. There is a reason: the little information leaked has shown this is a horrible idea for America. It allows Big Medicine to push generic and cheaper drugs out of the market for the sake of making people pay brand name prices. The TPP even subjects American businesses to international law as part of the bargain thereby undermining our nation's political process and protection of regular people. This deal stinks on ice.

It's another example of misaligned interests between government and the public.

This is utterly disgusting behavior from the people trusted to serve. They are not serving us, they're representing their big-money supporters and we get the short-end of the stick while they beat us over the head with the long-end of it.

The duties of elected representatives are to the people and to the truth. We need to vote out and replace those who don't understand this. Americans have the ability to do it now we must find the resolve. As a candidate with no party affiliation, I believe I am the best alternative Florida has to partisan politics as usual.

2   CAMPAIGN FINANCE

I am writing this book at a time just past the first anniversary of the "McCutcheon" Supreme Court decision which expanded areas of their prior "Citizens United" ruling. We have a system of government increasingly run by the few who not only possess the ability to buy political power, but also act on that ability.

I fully support a Constitutional amendment removing private money from politics, thereby making elections publicly funded. This would help level the playing field and allow more of the general public and regular, average people to become involved in our political process thereby loosening the chokehold big money currently has on us.

The Citizens United case shows just how far corruption runs up the political food chain. The result of the 5-4 split decision allows exorbitant sums of cash with no limitation to be given to candidates and committees in the name of "free speech." By its very definition "free" speech should not cost anything. The United States Supreme Court could not have ruled more in favor of the notion that "money talks." Overturning this travesty of justice, logic, and reason has widespread support and I also believe it is time for a full-blown Constitutional provision to start wiping out rampant political greed and "government for sale."

We have reached the point where campaign contributions, not the needs of our people, determine the legislation passed or even presented for consideration in Congress.

The extremely wealthy control the government through the financing of their puppets. Those greedy, little elected pawns won't stop the cash flow into their own pockets, therefore their efforts go to the highest bidders.

The wealthiest 14 (NOT 14%, but 14) people in the United States saw their wealth increase by $157 billion between 2013 and 2015. $157 billion is more money than is owned collectively by the bottom 128,000,000 Americans. The top one-tenth of the one percent rigs the system for their own gain. There was a time when assuming risk was rewarded, but there's little risk to be found for those running an already-rigged game. Kicking millions or even billions to help their stooges go campaigning is a mere pittance to them as they believe the pursuit of growing their own accounts and power should be at everyone else's expense.

It is my pledge that any funding my candidate committee accepts comes with the caveat to the donor that I am under no obligation to vote for or champion anything they believe in, want, or think they deserve. Contributors are therefore supporting exactly who they see because that is who they will get regardless of their monetary support or not. I make my positions well-known and I base my decisions on evidence. Aside from the evidence, the only other influences will be the wills and desires of the people of Florida. Those are the people I would be responsible to while defending the Constitution of our country. We must act to help people as a nation and not for the sake of the maladjusted interests of those currently in power. Current priorities are substantially misaligned.

People need and deserve jobs and living wages. Billionaires want even more tax breaks.

Citizens need and deserve health care. Multinational corporations want more tax cuts.

The people in the military need and deserve a raise and the ability to receive the care they've earned. The military-industrial complex wants more toys and politicians want more manufactured wars to use them in.

Those who are less-fortunate need Medicare, access to education, and affordable places to live. The greedy want more, more, and even more.

It is time for responsible leaders who know and respect the fact that the people are truly in charge and not the campaign contributors. Kick the insiders out who have promised a world full of favors or else we will just get more of the same and the sick cycle will remain intact.

Removing them and voting out those who don't believe we need campaign finance reform is the first step. Publicly funded elections can be financed from income tax check-offs (does not increase individual's tax liability) or add-ons (increases individual's liability). That way the pool of funds is spread and more people have access to active participation. Getting unlimited private money out of politics works toward leveling that playing field.

3   Education

Children

I have to jokingly admit there was a time when I could not stand children. All of the information I personally had confirmed my belief that they were all just germ-carrying pint-sized terrorists with the mission to break as many things as possible (at least that's how I was as a kid!). Being around my nieces and nephews when they were children always reinforced my stance (but seriously, they all grew up to be great adults).

My world changed when my then-girlfriend and her two daughters lived with me for a while. She would go to her work after I came home from mine and I would watch her girls (around 3 and 5 years old at the time) until she came home. They took to me practically instantly and I often felt like there were ducklings constantly following me around.

It was a totally new situation for me, but any trepidation I had vanished when I realized that I knew exactly how to deal with them. I recognized their type of behavior. I had seen it before. I knew how to handle it because kids are just like little, drunk adults. They're loud, messy, moody, in need of constant supervision, and half the things they say make absolutely no sense. I went to college and I used to speak in that language!

I like to joke, but the truth is they were hilarious and I'm so thankful because that time with my ex and her daughters completely changed my life. It made me fully realize that we all collectively owe it to these little people everywhere to improve the chances that they will have it better than we did. They have no clue what is going on in the big picture. Their heads are like pristine hard drives that adults seem to want to download their corrupted idea files into. We all need to protect and help them instead of limiting their chances. Regardless of if an individual has children or not, our society should value actively providing of our best efforts to successive generations in order to allow them the opportunity to thrive and grow. They are kids: they can't take care of themselves.

Currently, we are not acting in the best interests of children and it's incomprehensible. I couldn't explain to a child why we are still doing what we're doing. It makes no logical sense in today's age.

I want to show Falyn, Stella, Archer (my grandnieces and grandnephew), and young kids their age that we're trying to work hard for a brighter future. I don't want them to have to pay for even more bailouts in the future. Successive generations should thrive because of our work and not have to pay for the current system writing checks we can't cash. I want to show upcoming generations that there are people standing up and fighting for improving their chances and opportunities.

Primary Education

Why do we have a system for education? From an economic standpoint, we must educate new generations and pass our collective knowledge on to them as preparation for their eventual replacement of us in the workforce.

From a social standpoint, we need our fellow people to have as many useful skills and abilities in order to advance our society. Our odds of survival go up. We can't make it through life completely on our own as we are all dependent on each other in order for our nation and our society to even exist. Simply put, more people that have a clue about what they are doing and how to do it, the better off we all are.

We obviously need at least some organization to teaching and learning, therefore the question now involves the obligations we see inherent in a functional system. What exactly should we expect that system to do?

The duties of an efficient education system should

include educating a child's whole being. The extraordinary capabilities of children combined with the range and variety of human creativity have brought us to a place where we really have no idea what exactly is going to happen next or even what the near future will bring. Inventor and visionary Buckminster Fuller noticed that until 1900, collective human knowledge doubled approximately even century or so. By the end of 1950s, knowledge was doubling every quarter of a century. Today, on average, human knowledge is doubling every 13 months. According to IBM, the "internet of things" will lead to the doubling of knowledge every 12 hours.

Think how much and just how quickly the world has changed since you have been in elementary school. Our collective human knowledge is now growing at a previously unforeseen pace and can't be contained by archaic rules. This proves we must be flexible and not view an ever-changing world through the lenses of old ideas. No system can unconditionally guarantee the perfect conditions that will allow children to flourish, however, we must provide equality of opportunity for them to enter a level playing field. It increases the odds that we can collectively provide to children.

The education system should aim to prepare people to be productive and guide them to participate in a functioning society. However, not all current models are fully geared in that direction. Many were designed and implemented a very long time ago in a very different environment and have not changed dramatically since. Let's take a look at one such method of teaching.

The end of the Enlightenment Age and the entry into the industrial revolution in the late 18th century brought about massive educational change. Compulsory schooling paid for by taxes while free at the point of delivery was now in place for the first time in history.

The model they used tended to focus on deductive reasoning and knowledge of the classics. Using this strategy results in a split of people into the camps of "academic" or "non-academic." This artificial labeling leads many brilliant people to believe they are not because they are judged against a set of arbitrary academic standards. This system is currently in widespread use and the old routine of batching into groups and then processing through a system continues on. Age is not directly related to intelligence so grouping of students by ability for different tasks, projects, or assignments while in class makes more sense to me than combining into groups called "grades" and then waiting to see what happens in 12-13 years (results may vary).

Learning is not a simple linear progression. In reality, it seems like a lifelong process that more closely resembles an organism rather than a machine. Experts reject rigid systems and instead favor flowing, flexible, individualized and teaching.

Many schools take a linear approach and do so by emphasizing rote memorization. When they do, the typical procedure is to pass a standardized test then press on in-depth or move on to the next subject. This has the tendency to leave "Swiss-cheese gaps" in a student's knowledge and ability. Students can progress unimpeded through school even with these foundational gaps because it's only important to know what's on the test to end up passing. There should be no more, "teaching to the test" and no more high-stakes testing. Rote memorization can serve some purposes, but it should not comprise a complete approach. Instead, we should encourage mistakes, but expect mastery over time.

Intelligence is diverse, distinct, and dynamic. In order to form a more complete society, students must be able to learn to find their talents. This is in contrast with our current system which seems to have the prime directive of creating more university professors. We need to equip a more balanced hierarchy of math, science, arts, and communication.

Children should learn practical critical thinking skills from an early age. They should be taught to question, to defend their position, and to understand a position contrary to their own. There are no undeniably correct answers to the problems facing us, but through interaction, team dynamics, and their own peer review they can start to see how pieces of the real world puzzle start to come together. The answers are not at the back of the book. Self-awareness and personal responsibility are byproducts of critical thinking. Working knowledge and interaction need to replace short-term regurgitation of facts quantified through a multiple choice exam. Students should learn participation skills and initiative, which are two abilities completely lacking in many, most notably in politicians.

One role of the federal government is to establish standards that our nation's education system must meet or surpass. States should have leeway as there should never be a national curriculum to impose, but we need the states to produce results nonetheless.

An enormous problem exists in our method of testing. Standardized tests can play a vital role as a diagnostic tool, but not as an end-all be-all measure of learning. These types of tests allow educators to narrow down areas where students may need additional instruction and do a check on the spot. This is where technology comes into play enabling greater teaching to the individual. Sometimes, the private sector provides us with a great example of divergence from our current education model.

The non-profit Khan Academy is internationally known for its collection of thousands of videos covering everything from basic arithmetic, history, biology, to calculus and astrophysics. Sal Khan started putting the first YouTube videos up really just as a "kind of nice-to-have supplement" for his cousins. Millions of students and adults alike now use his site.

Khan says:

> "As soon as I put those first YouTube videos up something interesting happened- actually a bunch of interesting things happened. The first was feedback from my cousins. They told me they

preferred me on YouTube than in person. Once you get over the backhanded nature of that there is something very profound there. They were saying they preferred the automated version of their cousin to their cousin. At first it's very unintuitive, but when you actually think about it from their point of view, it makes a ton of sense. You have this situation where now they can pause and repeat their cousin without feeling like they're wasting my time. If they have to review something that they should have learned a couple of weeks ago, they don't have to be embarrassed and ask their cousin. They can just watch those videos. If they're bored, they can go ahead. They watch it at their own time at their own pace. And probably the least appreciated aspect of this is the notion that the very first time that you're trying to get your brain wrapped around a new concept the very last thing you need is another human being saying, 'Do you understand this?'

"The other thing that happened is, I put them on YouTube, I saw no reason to make it private, so I let other people watch it and then people started stumbling on it and I started getting some comments and some letters and all sorts of feedback from random people from around the world.

"And so you can imagine, here I was an analyst at a hedge fund. It was very strange for me to do something of social value."

This "Flipping the Classroom" approach could be used in every classroom in America tomorrow if lectures were assigned as homework and what was once known as homework becomes class work. Students do lower levels of cognitive work, such as gaining knowledge and comprehension, outside of class. In-class work involves using higher cognitive skills where they have support from peers and instructors.

Massive Open Online Courses (MOOCs) are web-based classes with no cap on participation. Anyone can join these courses as traditional learning materials like video lectures, readings, and corresponding problems are supplemented by interactive communities and forums used by students and instructors.

It's not a methodology, it's an ideology. These are just a few examples of using alternate strategies to produce superior results. There is nothing that is a perfect fix-all, but the more possibilities for less expensive ways of educating that we can get, the better.

Children from lower income families are at risk of falling on the wrong side of the digital divide. The 2009 stimulus package included $7.2 billion to bring more access to undeserved communities and the FCC announced the "Connect to Compete" program by which cable providers provide reduced cost internet access to lower income families. Plans to modernize the Lifeline program are progressing. We need to continue pushing for increased access and affordability of internet communication for people of all income levels. It's no longer a luxury, it's now a necessity.

Higher Education

The trend of college prices in the U.S. growing quicker than rates of inflation has existed since 1972. According to *The Economist*, education rates have spiraled out of control and are rising dramatically more than regular inflation, and that pace is even higher than health care inflation. It is indeed a sad state of affairs when college costs are outpacing the inflationary rise of bloated medical-related industries.

President Obama told his first joint session of Congress that, "Education is no longer a pathway to opportunity, it is a prerequisite." We have unfortunately bought into the notion that college is an absolute necessity. The Obama administration is now coming out with a way to measure and determine if you are "getting your money's worth" from college. Their intentions may be noble, but they completely miss on the issue since they see education as a private investment. We need to understand that education is a public good.

We're told to beg, borrow, steal, do whatever it takes to get into college and then when you get out everything will be better! However, the reality is that many start their post-college careers saddled with crippling debt and little to show for their money or their precious time. The earning power that was supposed to justify the assumption of student loans and offset their cost is rapidly diminishing. There was a time when jobs were all but guaranteed for college graduates but now there is simply less bang for your buck when it comes to higher education. What used to be a sound and prudent strategy is now an increasingly expensive gamble.

Data shows personal earning power is indeed higher if the person is a college graduate. However, it is becoming increasingly common to see the cost of higher education as being more than the benefit, at least when those furthering their education are getting less and less of what they pay for. If we do look at it from a "social goods" perspective, the price of higher education is much too high as it relates to what the return is. If we want to increase access to education, we must also have lower costs. Students and people wanting to further their education and development should be the last ones to suffer, but they are the ones bearing the brunt of an out of control system.

As of June 2015, $1.2 trillion of student debt exists in America. It's bad enough that Johnny can't read and Johnny can't write, but now Johnny can't repay his soul-crushing student loans.

Students obtain loans and then many can't repay. When they can't repay, their credit ratings take hits, followed by wage and tax refund garnishments. This in turn hurts their employment chances and directly drives down the country's potential. Students are being forced to pay for their own torture devices by the very lenders peddling the lie that they're only there to help. In reality, lenders are only there to make a profit.

One of the biggest perpetrators is the for-profit

university sector, including the University of Phoenix. A 2012 report from the Senate Committee on Health, Education, Labor, and Pensions (HELP) found that the 15 largest for-profit education companies received 86% of their revenue from federal aid of some form and those schools went on to spend $3.7 billion on marketing and advertising. According to ESPN, from 2006 through 2026, the University of Phoenix will spend $154.5 million for the naming rights of the Arizona Cardinals' stadium. It may seem like a paltry sum considering their over $2.6 billion net revenue in 2014 alone, but it's something I would think about before writing a tuition check. Additionally, the HELP report found the University of Phoenix spent an average $2,225 on marketing per student in 2010, while it only spent $892 per student on instruction.

The Department of Education has the power to address the problem. Congress has given them the power to administer student loan programs and the authority to collect on those loans. They also have broad authority to reduce or forgive those debts. Under the Higher Education Act, the Department of Education has the ability to cancel loan repayment if colleges lied to the borrower or undermined the quality of students' educations or finances. One qualification for forgiveness is being lured by predatory lenders using misleading job placement rates.

Another qualification which could prompt loan forgiveness is if a college shuts its doors, which was going to be the case of for-profit Corinthian University after it was found to have doctored job placement data. The result was a cutoff of the Department of Education subsidies. Corinthian was even sued by the Consumer Financial Protection Bureau and is still currently battling the lawsuit. Tens of thousands of Corinthian students' federal loans are still on the government's balance sheet after federal officials brokered a deal in which ECMC, a student-debt collector with a reported history of aggressive collection tactics, took over Corinthian's 50 plus campuses. Robyn Smith, an attorney for the National Consumer Law Center, notes that Corinthian could ultimately share in profits from a successful buyout. Is the Higher Education Act meant to guarantee affordable and equal access or is it simply a tool to help generate profit while ignoring deceptive practices?

The Coalition for Educational Success is a lobbying group representing for-profit colleges and their parent companies. President Obama tried to end the practice of giving federally-guaranteed loans to those schools with histories of combining high student loans and providing lousy job prospects. In 2010 alone, the Coalition for Educational success spent $8 million on lobbying and kicked back $2 million in campaign contributions and successfully weakened any regulation potentially coming out of the President's proposal. Over three hundred members of the bought-sold-and-paid-for Congress threatened to defund the Department of Education if the federal cutoff of predatory institutions went through. Greed won again.

Colleges and universities are also in an academic arms race to jack up rates in pursuit of the almighty "Prestige Factor." The name of the institution on your diploma often carries much more weight than the quality or the substance of your actual education. When universities feel a drop in prestige they in turn hire so-called star professors, and those professors don't come cheaply. Fancy buildings are sure to follow. That cost is then passed down to students. Competition for this abstract Prestige Factor erodes value. It is another example of students paying more for less.

One of the reasons prompting me to leave Stetson Law School is my calculation that at the end of my courses I would have over $120,000 of debt. Burdened with that debt I would then have to compete in a completely oversaturated legal market with no decent odds of even a $30,000 a year job. Highly illogical doesn't even begin to describe that situation.

Interest rates on Federal Stafford Loans are fixed. The current interest rates for new Federal Stafford Loans in 2014-2015 are 4.66% for undergraduate students and 6.21% for graduate and professional students. The federal funds rate is the primary tool that the Federal Open Market Committee uses to influence interest rates and the economy. The federal funds rate is the borrowing cost of banks in the overnight lending market when they borrow money from other banks, essentially creating money out of thin air. Are you sitting down? Currently, and for the past year, the federal funds target rate is only 0% to 0.25% and has been consistently around 0.12%. Banks enjoy much lower borrowing rates than someone trying to further their education. These are the same banks that demand to be bailed out and add fuel to the fire of market collapse. The system is rigged, and it's not in the favor of the people. The current setup obviously doesn't benefit America as a whole.

We need leadership that will stand up for those being fleeced and that leadership sure isn't coming from the bought-off Republican Party or those who qualify as part of the paid-for political left.

We shouldn't punish the people who hit the books trying to give themselves and their families a better chance. They've paid dearly and their families have also. Factor in the time value and economic value and the only conclusion is that students are being horribly underserved.

Toward Solutions

We obviously need to change the course we're on. Our workforce needs to become more adept at being creative and tapping into those abilities involves education starting at an early age. Creativity is the process of producing original ideas that have value. The more ways that an individual can see and interpret a problem the more likely they are to be able to come up with actual viable solutions. Young people with practical working knowledge and practice in group dynamics add to our society's aggregate potential. Solid critical thinking skills they will need for the future are built upon a multi-dimensional approach to solving problems instead using an ancient linear progression to get an answer. Answers and explanations in real life are not found at the back of the book.

Flexibility is also vital in the rapidly evolving and increasingly connected world as it allows you to change your own actions and direction. Increased adaptability, or the ability to respond quickly to change, results when circumstances beyond your control happen and you must adjust. Young people should have a strong understanding of flexibility by the time they enter higher levels of learning.

Creativity, open-mindedness, flexibility, and adaptability are vital abilities needed in the constantly changing world and business climate. Education system administration should provide parameters between which the job needs to be done, but they must give the teachers and instructors actually doing the job the ability and leeway to do it. Micromanaging has never solved anything and only makes matters worse.

Teachers and educators should be actively consulted and relied upon when states organize their education systems. There's not a lot of money in solving problems, but education reformers make a lot more money by prolonging those problems. One company that appears to be in the "right place at the right time" is Pearson. Pearson is a London-based mega-corporation that owns everything from the Financial

Times to Penguin Books and dominates the mega-business of educating America's children. It appears that Pearson has successfully greased the democratic process in their favor and through connections to seedy American Legislative Exchange Council (ALEC), has now become the dominant provider of educational resources and services in the K-12 and post-secondary markets.

We must redraw the blurred line between private firms churning a profit and the education system. Education in America should be viewed as a public good. Being mandated to use a company's process which is clearly designed to sell even more books, supporting materials, or online program access is despicable. We need to restore and rebuild the public school sector and get profit based companies out of the education business. The non-profit Khan Academy is proof that the private sector can provide wonderful services to people without creating a giant, sucking, unbreakable profiteering loop. The less control that for-profit companies have on education, the more control and power that teachers, parents, and students regain.

Just as corporations shouldn't tell instructors how to teach, standards shouldn't either. The federal government is responsible for adjusting what qualifies as a minimal set of standards and the goal should be to raise those standards over time, but it is up to the states to implement their systems to help us collectively get there using federal assistance where appropriate.

STEAM teaching systems can be used as that

methodology involves using math and science to solve real-world challenges and problems. It is an applied, project-based way of teaching and learning that allows students to understand and appreciate the relevancy of their work and how it connects to the world around them. Arts education is a key to creativity and STEAM approaches include it. When looking at a complete model, physical education (P.E.) should definitely be included. Real world abilities grow from applied-learning and it provides a platform for developing skills for all types of students and not just those who intend to go to college and beyond. Having more people with more skill and aptitude greatly enhances America's financial, economic, and social strength.

Artificial limits on grade levels can restrict some advanced students while dragging others along even though they may not be ready. Ending age segregation allows students to master different areas of learning at different speeds and at different ages. Younger students learn from older students and older students learn through teaching to younger children all while under the facilitation and guidance of a teacher.

People with varied skills and abilities will help address the growing skills gap in America. Granted, some industries do not suffer from this gap, however the ones that do are hurting. In its 2013 report titled, "Talent Shortage Survey Research Results," staffing company Manpower states that regardless of size, 2 of every 5 businesses are having major problems finding qualified workers. Their analysis elaborates, "A lack of candidates with technical competencies such as professional qualifications and skilled trades experience are the most common explanations for talent shortages in the Americas." Brilliant tradespeople are essential and allowing people to explore their talents enhances those abilities.

A great deal of Federal student loan forgiveness must occur. Those advancing their education will be able to go forward without the weight of enormous loan repayments. Students suffer when colleges create their own bloated budget monstrosities and pass them the buck. I believe every college should disclose its spending in an open audit system available for the public to inspect and review online. Downward pressure on the price of higher education will allow more actual earning power after college, thus creating more take home pay which benefits producers because consumers actually now have money to use to buy their products.

Students and families will have more money to spend and stimulate the economy. Tax revenue from that spending and boost to the economy will offset some of the loss of the revenue inflow the government would have received had they not written off loans. Cuts in other parts of the budget will replace some more of that difference. The housing sector will also be positively affected as more can actually afford housing or to upgrade their living conditions.

Generations in our education system are being packaged up, processed, and then thrown out ill-prepared to excel. They've been instructed to operate in conformity so they can fit into a world that doesn't exist anymore. We certainly have the ability to help them, but we must collectively create a massive effort to change the current composition and overarching strategy of our collective education system. We cannot afford simple education reform, we need to go full-on education system revolution if we are going to compete in the 21st century.

4   OUR ENVIRONMENT, ANIMALS, AND PURPLE DOG ANIMAL SANCTUARY

Earthly Matters

As far as we know, Earth is the only place in the universe to harbor life. We are doing an increasingly horrible job at protecting and preserving the place.

The evidence is overwhelming that our planet is undergoing detrimental climate change and humans are accelerating the pace. There are those who are myopic and so immune to facts that they deny it is happening and are so selfish that they would rather cater to special interests for money. We need to take action before it's too late. A shift toward a Public versus Private mentality will allow us to operate for the betterment of our environment.

A critic is correct when he or she says the Earth is not going anywhere no matter what we do. Earth isn't going anywhere... we are. If we abuse nature past the breaking point Earth will essentially shake us off like a bad case of fleas or just another closed-end biological mistake. There is no indication help will come from elsewhere to save us from ourselves so we must change our attitudes, our practices, and ourselves.

I see a Florida by 2030 that gets at very least 15% of its energy needs from solar power. We currently receive 2% due in part to the repeal of solar rebates in 2014 after the efforts of state energy company lobbyists. If "The Sunshine State" is advertised as our nickname, maybe we should live up to it. We need to stress pro-solar legislation at every turn. Lobbyists for unclean energies will not give up their push so we need to fight even harder. We must protect clean water and make fines, sanctions, penalties, and prosecution of polluters a reality. There are no justifiable excuses for why offenders are getting away with outright crime.

I find it reprehensible that people lack access to clean drinking water. With all of the totally exorbitant luxuries that some have I see no way how they could possibly justify polluting or removing the ability for the public to have safe water.

We should increase revenue by instituting an annually rising national carbon tax as we move away from the dirtiest of fuels and power. Economist Laura D'Andrea Tyson wrote on June 2013:

> "The beauty of a carbon tax is its market-based
> simplicity. Economists since Adam Smith have
> insisted that prices are by far the most efficient

way to guide the decisions of producers and consumers. Carbon emissions have an 'unpriced' societal cost in terms of their deleterious effects on the earth's climate. A tax on carbon would reflect these costs and send a powerful price signal that would discourage carbon emissions."

The Congressional Budget Office says a $20 per ton tax that raises 5.6% a year would raise $1.2 trillion over a decade.

There is no other place that humans can migrate to. There is no other place we can colonize and settle yet. Like it or not, the Earth is where we make our stand. We need to cherish and preserve the only home we've ever known.

I am a huge supporter of animal rights so I also plan a review of the USDA's policies and procedures regarding the apparent oversight and lack of fines and inspections that would help curb abuse. There are multitudes of varying state laws concerning animal rights and the USDA is tasked with many aspects of enforcement at the federal end (such as site inspections), but there are gaps between those state and federal laws and regulations. By closing the divisions we can be more effective in protecting animals. We will also expand some of the Animal Welfare Act of 1966 to give it more punch. I also support closing loopholes in current puppy mill laws.

Purple Dog Animal Sanctuary

I've been lucky to have been around animals my entire life. I learned to love, respect, and care for animals because of my family's long history with them.

Here are just a few random examples of the many animals my family has taken care of: In the late 1970s my mom noticed a bizarre little creature that seemed lost in the middle of a blizzard in Dayton, Ohio. It turned out to be a stray rat terrier that she and my sisters named Phyllis (after Phyllis Diller because of her crazy hair). Phyllis lived a long life, somewhere around 16 to 18 years.

Koyak the Pekingese was my best friend growing up. My mom said she would never buy from a pet store, but she happened to see the saddest little Pekingese in a little cage with just a bowl. Koyak, like Phyllis, lived for around 18 years or so. We've had so many different animals all with unique personalities I can't even keep track of all of them!

My mom and family also rescued wild animals, helped them get healthy, and then released them. One blue jay kicked out of its nest even had to be released twice. This little guy loved to be fed with baby food on the end of a paintbrush. Alvin was so smart he learned to mimic the telephone that was next to him because people would come over to answer and he wanted the attention a ring brought. The first time my mom released him one of Florida's notorious afternoon thunderstorms popped up out of nowhere and Alvin responded by jumping from branch to branch with his mouth wide open to the sky. For as smart as he was, he had no concept of drowning. She brought him back in and later on that week he was released again, this time he was able to fly off. There have been a few more birds like him that she rescued, but that little dude was special. Squirrels kicked out of the nest were also no stranger to mom's rescues and one named Muldoon even had a back leg in a tiny cast for a short bit while he healed.

My sister, Tricia, also cared for animals deeply. She worked in a veterinarian's office and volunteered at Eglin Air Force Base's Pet Welfare Shelter. Tricia would also take the feral and stray cats from the woods behind our house to the vet to have them spayed or neutered and then release them back into the wild.

To this day, my dad still mixes plates of different dry and wet cat foods (even with a little bit of ham and cheese!) to feed many of those same strays that hang out around the back yard. His house is at the end of a cul-de-sac and apparently has some mythical kind of strong magnetic animal force! So many stray dogs and cats ended up there.

Of course I've loved all of our dogs, but the funniest one I've had was Lucy Liu, the Rottweiler-dachshund. No kidding, the Humane Society of Tampa Bay volunteers outside of PetSmart running the adoptions informed us the dachshund was the father. Her pops must have been one brave wiener-dog. I have no idea how that conception worked logistically, but it resulted in one great pup. You know you have a unique dog when your first reaction is, "What the %#&@ is that thing!" Her big barreled body and stubby legs never stopped her from tearing around the yard chasing lizards. I don't think she ever caught one, but she would never give up trying.

Lucy Liu was one dog out of the many of our pets, each one special in their own ways. Animals have given me so many great memories I want to give something back to them.

I founded Purple Dog Animal Sanctuary, a 501 (c) (3) public charity, to tackle 3 needs. The first is to provide a home for abandoned senior dogs (with the intent of expansion for other animals in the future). Secondly, to reduce traditional energy reliance by using efficient methods and repurposed material to promote the sustainability embodied in rammed-Earth mass technology. Thirdly, to do so at low cost to encourage others to develop and build similar structures.

My vision is to start at a relatively small scale and over time develop a multi-use public complex around a thriving and self-sufficient animal sanctuary. Luckily, before I am even able to break ground on the sanctuary I'm in a favorable starting position because a similar (but a bit more complex) building design has already been approved under Florida and Universal Building Codes and was being built by others in neighboring Manatee County (I live in Sarasota County).

The actual design, construction, and approach of Purple Dog Animal Sanctuary draws from numerous existing technologies and systems invented, refined, and furthered by architect Michael Reynolds. I've used his books and so much information from others to derive plans and specifications adapted for Purple Dog.

I am not afraid to use non-conventional methods to meet needs. A typical brick and mortar process can be costly, wasteful, and energy inefficient in the long run. We shouldn't be scared of going off the beaten path. By showing others how the process works I will help promote both energy-saving construction as well as provide a place where older dogs can live out their days or be adopted to forever homes.

I will go into a bit of depth here in the book to demystify a lot of the construction and maintenance and to show what has inspired many to build in this environmentally responsible manner. I also encourage you to take a look at various websites to see just how colorful and beautiful many of the interiors are.

The designs I am using make use of are based on techniques developed by Michael Reynolds. He currently lives in New Mexico, but this architectural journey started when graduated from the University of Cincinnati in 1969. *The Architectural Record* published his thesis in 1971 and he built his first recycled material house in 1972. That house, affectionately known as his "Thumb House" because of its profile, actually used empty beer cans wired together into "bricks." Those bricks were then mortared together in a patented process. The entire process has been refined dramatically in over four decades worth of hard work, dealing with political bureaucracy, and revolutionizing material use and construction techniques.

Reynolds says he had an epiphany the moment when he realized that practically any object, whether it be an old bottle or used tires, could not only become part of the building structure but could also be used for their insulating properties. He has written five books concerning "Earthship Biotecture." *Stephen Fry in America* showed Fry receiving a guided tour of Reynolds' home and information about how the Earthship systems work. A 2007 documentary, *Garbage Warrior*, highlights his life and work.

In Garbage *Warrior,* Michael Reynolds describes one model design called The Phoenix:

> "There's nothing coming into this house, no power lines, no gas lines, no sewage lines coming out, no water lines coming in, no energy being used… We're sitting on 6,000 gallons of water, growing food, sewage internalized, 70 degrees (21 degrees Celsius) year-round… What these kind of houses are doing is taking every aspect of your life and putting it into your own hands… A family of four could totally survive without having to go to the store."

The name "Earthship" was coined by Reynolds' wife, Chris. It is so named because like a ship, it is meant to be a self-contained, operable "vessel." Over time, Earthships were able to become off-grid relying on solar power, geothermal cooling, growing food, and water cycling through greywater and black water systems. "Earthship" is a registered trademark of Michael Reynolds and his organization and home are located in Taos, New Mexico.

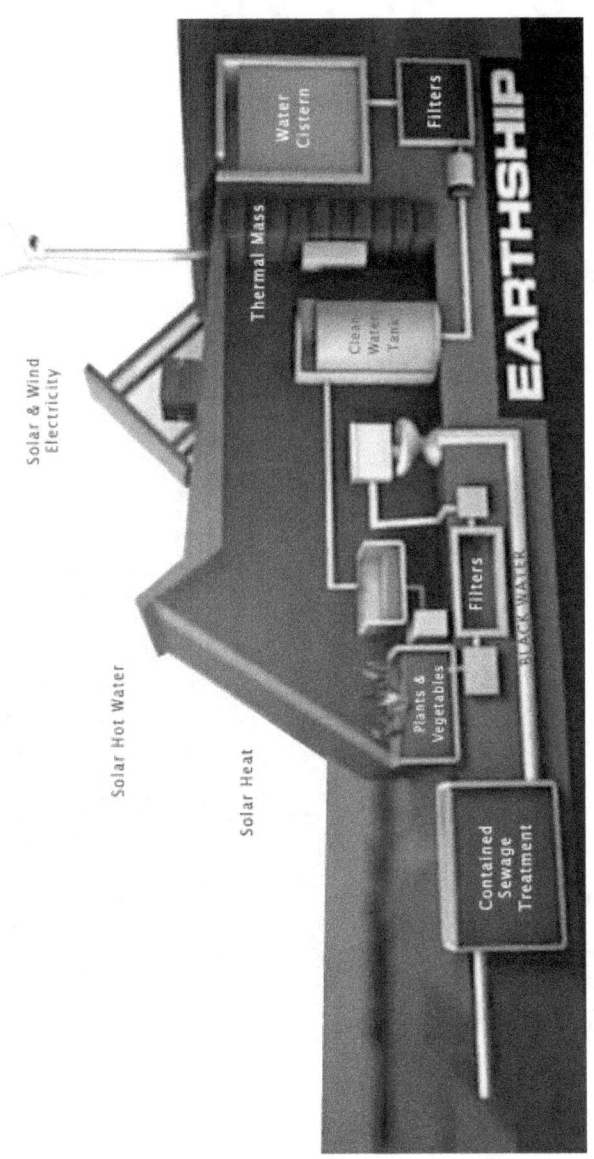

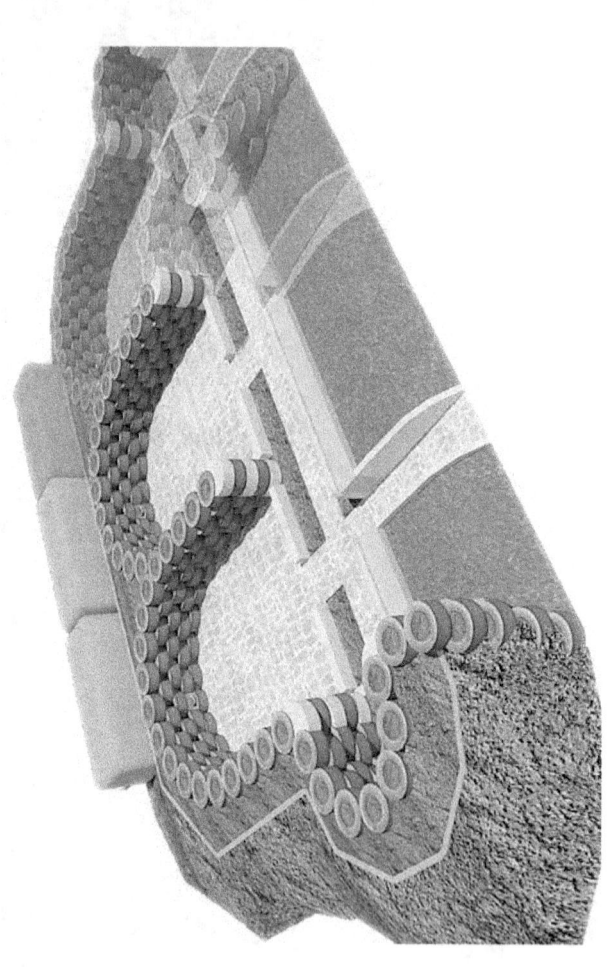

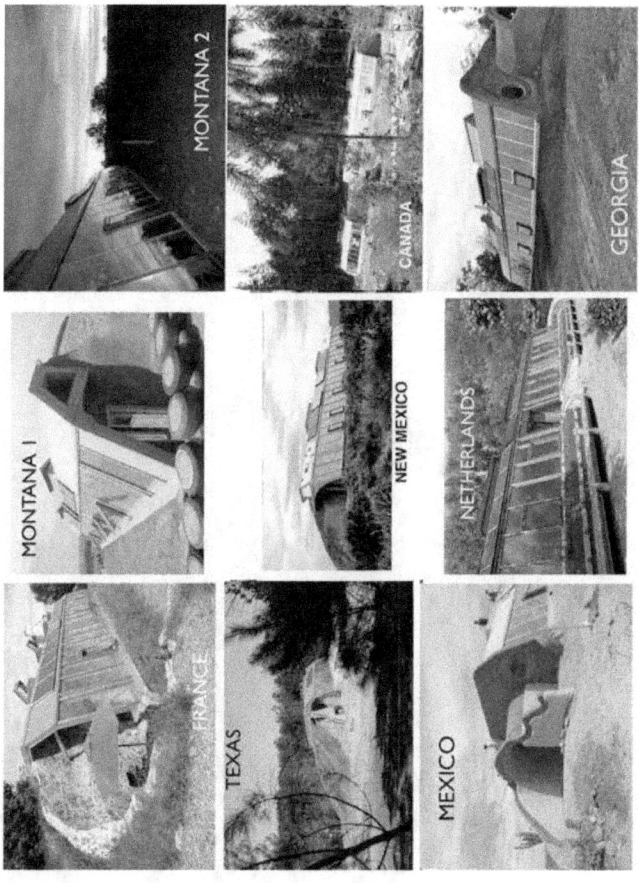

Environmental activists and celebrities became interested and Reynolds was even commissioned by actors Keith Carradine and Dennis Weaver to build high-end models.

Current Earthship technology uses Rammed Earth Masses to regulate interior temperature. Used automobile tires are rammed with native dirt to provide both structure and natural insulation. Each rammed tire ends up weighing approximately 300 pounds. This thermal mass construction combined with natural cross ventilation and the stack effect (thermal draft or chimney effect) of moving air provides natural heating and cooling while maintaining comfortable temperatures inside.

Another wonderful aspect of Earthships is their adaptability to any climate. At least 17 countries have Earthships. They range from frigid Canada, with minus 30 degree temperatures, to hot and humid areas like Haiti. Japan and France have joined the club as well.

There are usually a few concerns people have when they learn about such a design. First, we all know tire fires are notoriously difficult to extinguish. However, the tires in Earthships do not burn since they are not in piles and there is no access to the oxygen that fires need to burn as the walls over the tires are fully plastered and/or finished with concrete, adobe, or other covering. The Hondo Fire of New Mexico in 1996 hit an Earthship and the tire portion of the structure remained intact and did not ignite whatsoever.

Outgassing from the tires initially worries some.

However, technical reports conclude there is nothing to worry about because as these are used tires, they have been exposed to the elements for years and there is no threat of harm.

Earthships are not only designed to meet building codes but also to exceed performance required in the Uniform Building Code (UBC) adopted in most states. From Earthship.com:

"Building codes and lending institutions basically control the type of housing that is available or possible. This is because building permits and financing must be obtained prior to building. Most new or different concepts have to be rigorously proven to the building code officials as officials are not being paid to take risks on new ideas. They are being paid to enforce existing dogma. Consequently, they tend to go by the existing books regardless of environmental or human issues to make sure they don't lose their jobs.

"To further complicate the matter, the lending institutions do not necessarily accept any approvals of new ideas by the building code officials anyway. Their objective is to secure the resale value of the dwelling to cover themselves in case of default by the borrower. Consequently, they stick to things that have been proven to re-sell over the years, regardless of whether they are appropriate for the planet or for the people.

"Every state follows the same Uniform Building Code. This code has a clause that allows for alternative methods "not covered in this document." It states that alternative methods must meet the requirements and standards of those presented in the UBC. Your objective would, therefore, be to illustrate that Earthship Biotecture meets and exceeds the standards put forth in the UBC. In New Mexico, this has already been done. If you plan to build in New Mexico you are home free as far as the codes and permits go.

"Every state has a different policy on how approvals are handled. For example, New Mexico has a statewide policy. If something is approved by the state office it holds true all over the state. Colorado, (where many Earthships have been built), has a county by county policy which means that each county has the power to interpret alternative methods as they see fit. This means that if one county approves, it does not necessarily mean that the next one will. Several counties in Colorado have approved of this concept. No one has rejected it."

Today's Earthships use U-shaped walls, which provide excellent stability. The walls are backfilled on the exterior to provide additional strength and insulation. Smaller tires can be used in higher courses in the wall and each additional higher row is staggered back approximately an inch to allow for even more structural integrity.

The ends of the walls are further bolstered by concrete half blocks. The tops of tire walls are "can and concrete bond beams" made of recycled cans and concrete, or wooden bond beams with wooden shoes attached using concrete anchors attached to poured blocks of concrete inside of the top tires.

Non-load bearing interior walls can be made of a honeycomb pattern of aluminum cans joined by concrete. The walls are then plastered with adobe or concrete finishing.

Earthship design allows for catching, storing, and using water from the local environment, whether it be snow, rain, or condensation. Water enters a silt-catching filter, then flows into a cistern. Gravity then allows the water to flow through a water organization module (WOM) that filters out contaminants and bacteria producing safe water for drinking. The WOM has a conventional direct current (DC) pump which pushes the water to a pressure tank in order to create regular water pressure throughout the structure for sinks, showers, and more.

Toilets do not use water directly from the WOM, they use greywater. Greywater is water that has been used already (from the sinks, showers, etc.). Before it gets to the toilets though, the greywater is channeled through grease filters and particle digester and into a rubber-lined botanical cell. This water is unsuitable for drinking, but plant life thrives on it. After passing through the botanical cell and watering plants the greywater flows to the toilets for use in flushing.

After use in toilets, the resulting water is referred to as black water. Septic tanks and a leach field or drain field further make use of the water as exterior plants away from the Earthship structure love the nutrients in black water. Like with water, Earthships are designed to collect and store their own energy as well. The majority of electricity comes from photovoltaic solar panels. Wind turbines can also supplement power production. DC energy is then stored in deep-cycle batteries. If needed, integration with the standard grid can be done.

It is standard practice to use a Power Organizing Module (POM) to take stored energy from the deep-cycle batteries and invert it for alternating current (AC) use. The POM is simply placed on an interior wall and wired completely conventionally. Standard circuit breakers and converters allow the energy to be used for appliances through everyday outlets.

Earthships make use of balancing solar heat gain from windows, thermal energy retention in the walls and soil, and natural ventilation for cooling. The collective thermal mass of the rammed-Earth mass walls absorbs heat during the day and radiates it at night providing even temperatures without additional electricity for air conditioning or powered heaters.

Ventilation is enhanced by cooler air coming in through a front "hopper" window and air flow coming from buried air tubes. The air drawn inward through the tubes due to the chimney effect (stack effect) is naturally cooled before it enters the structure because the piping is underground where the soil is substantially colder than the surface. The result is a natural air conditioner with streaming fresh air.

Earthships have been built throughout the world. Locations in Europe include Scotland, France, the Netherlands, Portugal, Belgium, Spain, Sweden, Estonia, and the Czech Republic.

African sites include South Africa, Sierra Leone, Malawi, and Swaziland. Other areas around the globe featuring Earthship technology are Easter Island, the Philippines, Canada, Mexico, Haiti, Jamaica, Belize, and Guatemala.

The largest concentrations of Earthships in the United States are in New Mexico and Colorado, but other notable Earthships are in Texas, Georgia, Montana, and one partially built in Manatee County, Florida.

The 21st century brings problems of both type and magnitude the likes of which we haven't seen. We need creative ideas and methods to solve them more than ever. The building technique I'm using for Purple Dog Animal Sanctuary demonstrates just one way I don't blindly accept the status quo.

5   FINANCE, ECONOMICS, AND INTERNATIONAL TRADE

The Scum of Wall Street Runs Deep

I'd like to describe Wall Street as a deep pond with only a bit of scum on the top, but in reality it seems to be a cesspool of feces littered with the rotting corpses of morality and ethics. These are the type of people who would step over homeless families in the street if it meant more time to write new business. The financial industry is increasingly lawless and is fleecing more from America's hardworking people than ever before.

Workers' wages are stagnant, but Wall Street bonuses for the people who don't even make anything tangible (except for a mess that taxpayers have to clean up) are at all-time high. They're even getting paid for betting the wrong way on massive financial gambles. Five years after the Dodd-Frank financial reform was signed into law, regulators have still not enacted Section 956. That section prohibits executive pay tied to taking "inappropriate risks."

Wall Street bonuses in 2014 totaled $28,500,000,000 (for 167,800 employees) whereas the annual earnings of all full-time minimum wage workers (just over 1 million of them) COMBINED equaled LESS THAN HALF of that. Wall Street is off the deep end.

Even though I worked in the financial industry and own Purple Dog Financial, Inc., I do not have any blood on my hands. I ceased operations when I learned and discovered even more about how rampant greed is at every turn in the industry and cannot stomach their practices.

During my time with financial firms I focused on nonaggressive presentations dealing with Social Security, risk management, and college savings plans. I believe there's a lot to be said about attraction versus overbearing promotion. I strongly rejected being prodded by to sell annuities or interrupt people door-to-door to sell a commodity such as Medicare supplements. Ethics and morals do not seem to mesh with the financial industry very well. Even after being told to focus on the affluent market I still focused on normal people.

CEOs and executives are getting away with abuse and bloody murder. Prudent investments with reasonable and justifiable returns were once normal, but now rampant swings in speculative investments are standard. Something went grossly and horribly wrong along the way.

Timeline

I will go into more depth and description of some of these events and their importance throughout the next portion of the book:

1791   -Congress creates the First U.S. Bank

1816   -The Second Bank of the U.S. is chartered

1833-1836   -Second Bank of the U.S. increases the money supply by 84%
- Total supply grows from $150 million to $267 million

1837-1843   -Panic of 1837 and depression ensues
- 194 of 729 banks in U.S. close

1907   -Banking Panic of 1907
- The New York Stock Exchange plummets as panicked bank customers across America withdraw money. Bankers secretly back the formation of the Federal Reserve even though they originally publicly denounce it.

1908	-Nelson Aldrich Heads new National Monetary Commission
	• Senate Republican Nelson Aldrich heads a commission tasked with studying how the financial collapse happened. Aldridge has close ties with J.P. Morgan and his daughter married John D. Rockefeller.
1910	-Bankers privately meet on Jekyll Island, Georgia
	• They plan for over a week drafting a proposal for a private banking system. Attendees include Nelson Aldrich, A.P. Andrew (Assistant Secretary of the Treasury), Frank Vanderlip (President of National City Bank of New York), Charles D. Norton (President of J.P. Morgan-dominated First National Bank of New York), Paul Warburg (Kuhn, Loeb, & Company), Henry Davidson (Senior Partner of J.P. Morgan) and Benjamin Strong (representing J.P. Morgan).

1913   -Federal Reserve Act passes
- Two days before Christmas, while many Congressmen were on vacation, the central banking system we have today was created. It allows banks to essentially create money out of thin air by loaning money to borrowers with interest payable back to the lender.

-16th Amendment is ratified, establishing income taxation
- From that point on, taxpayers are legally on the hook for paying for central bank failings and debt collections.

1914   -Federal Reserve banks open

1915   -J.P. Morgan and Co. profit from war
- A deal is made with the Bank of England and a monopoly on underwriting war bonds in the United Kingdom and France is established. They also invest in war equipment suppliers.

1921-1929 -Federal Reserve increases the money supply by 62%
- Artificial boom is created when $28 billion enters the market.

1929 -Federal Reserve contracts the money supply
- The Fed starts by pulling dollars out of the money supply, thus creating an inevitable bust after issuing so much credit previously. The Fed's actions trigger another banking crisis leading to the Great Depression.

-"Black Thursday" stock market crash
- The most devastating plunge consolidates billions of value in the hands of private brokers at the expense of everyone else.

1930 -The Great Depression begins

1933 -The Federal Reserve finishes contracting the money supply by 33% since 1929

1963 -President Kennedy threatens the Federal Reserve's money monopoly
- Executive Order 11110

authorizes the Treasury to issue silver certificates. This government-issue currency bypasses the need of the government to borrow from bankers at interest.

1999   -Financial Services Modernization Act

- Economists recognize that this played an enormous part in the financial crisis. It repealed part of the Glass-Steagall Act of 1933 and thereby allowed investment banks, commercial banks, insurance companies, and securities firms to merge. Citigroup had merged with Travelers Insurance and needed a way to keep the company together. The government allowed Citi officials to review and write drafts. Robert Rubin, Secretary of the Treasury, helped move the resulting legislation (more about Rubin in the next section).

2000-2003   -Federal Reserve lowers the Federal Funds Rate from 6.5% to 1%

- They set up another boom.

2004   -Investment banks and Securities and Exchange Commission (SEC) cut a deal

- Five of the largest investment banks, including Bear Stearns and Goldman Sachs (they run by Henry Paulson, who later became Secretary of the Treasury) met with the SEC and convinced them that banks should be allowed to self-regulate and determine for themselves how much money they could make out of thin air and then loan. This is called the bank's leverage ratio. The SEC agreed and unleashed billions of dollars for high-risk investment packages. Not long after, the economy collapsed, resulting in more wealth and power consolidation for private bankers (who in essence run the Federal Reserve).

2004-2006   -Federal Reserve contracts the market

- The bust starts by making loans and adjustable rate mortgages become more expensive. Fed raises Federal Funds rate to 5.25%.

2007-2010   -Worst financial crisis since the Great
                 Depression

- Globally, millions lost homes, jobs, and retirement funds. Large banks absorbed smaller ones, thus furthering the consolidation of wealth and reducing competition. J.P. Morgan Chase bought Washington Mutual (the biggest bank to fail in the United States).

2010   -Banks report record profits

- This includes J.P. Morgan Chase with a record profit of $17.4 billion that year.

The Rise of Inequality and Our Current Condition

As you can see by just some of those important dates, America's financial history has been a series of boom and bust cycles mixed with some extremely sketchy backroom dealings. With so much of the world's financial wealth (the shrinking portion not currently being privately hoarded) tied up in an increasingly volatile mix of investment speculation and gambling, the next major bust will be absolutely crippling. We draw down the odds of disaster and the magnitude of impact by managing risk responsibly and not going all-in on unsuitable investments or allowing supermassive wealth concentration. How much inequality can we tolerate and still have an economy that works for everyone while maintaining a functional democracy?

In the 1960s and 1970s the wealthiest 1 percent of Americans received 9 to 10 percent of the nation's income. Just before the 2008 financial crisis that share went to 23.5 percent. The richest one-tenth of 1 percent tripled their wealth over the same time period. Meanwhile, average worker wages have stagnated and experienced an under 1 percent gain (adjusted for inflation) over a third of a century, and in 2001 the median wage actually dropped.

There is nothing inherently wrong with having wealth. However, how you acquire it and how much you feel you actually need do matter. Even if you temporarily overlook those points and the numerous moral arguments that can easily be made by hoarding so much when so many people have so little, economically speaking, there is no way we can have something remotely resembling a functional economy without a stable and thriving middle class.

We currently have extreme inequality and it is made worse because America's large middle class has less and less purchasing power and often has to go into debt to try to make ends meet. Middle America has not recovered. That's why no one really feels any decrease in financial burden despite better economic numbers and news. Not only is middle class purchasing power down, but people are finding they can no longer rely on borrowing, either.

Extreme income inequality has roots in our policy changes. Not everyone who has a massive amount of money is trying to run and influence the government, but more and more political clout is bought by those who have the money in order to gain influence, votes, and produce specific outcomes. Societal issues and economic dysfunction result when money becomes concentrated in fewer and fewer hands while wages in the middle class stay stagnant. Compounding occurs when gains in wealth are not reinvested in jobs and growth.

Large corporations are often the biggest moochers. They avoid taxes and get bailed out with taxpayer funds when they screw up. They are bound by fewer and fewer regulations and swindling CEOs get away clean with everything from extortion to ineptitude to fleecing consumers.

When big corporations dodge taxes it leads to shrinking government revenue and results in fewer public services and deteriorating public schools, unsafe bridges, declining roads, and much more.

It also leads to even more Americans competing ever more fiercely for an ever-shrinking piece of the pie. Workers are receiving less of the share for their production efforts and have to fight for employment in a shrinking job pool. Middle class Americans are now competing with poorer Americans for the same jobs and resources. Dwindling public resources make matters worse. Politics: now cynical to the breaking point and mean beyond any measure of sanity.

The system has run amok, but there are a few key fundamentals to remember. Capitalism does great things. It was never invented per se, but instead developed out of the ways people dealt with each other. Capitalism does need some inequality to function as this incentivizes the pursuit of improving your standard of living. Efficiency and production of in-demand goods are often justly rewarded. However, big corporations have thrown this conventional capitalism to the wayside in favor of disaster capitalism.

Capitalism is obviously our best and only option, but it needs to be tamed because people are being allowed to get away with murder. They're too big to fail and never get jailed because none of the rules somehow apply to them. We've already established that when Wall Street gets another bailout the taxpayers are stuck picking up the tab. How much are the bankers going to cry for next time? When will it ever be enough for them? Regular Americans are understandably sharpening their pitchforks.

Trickle-down economics is the worst economic lie ever sold. Republicans have been spouting it for years, but there was a time when Democrats would stand up to them and call out the falsities. There was a very noticeable shift of when the Democrats could no longer validly claim to be helping the middle class and it came through deregulation and trade dealings as the party picked up camp and moved several steps over to the right.

Bill Clinton and Robert Rubin: A Bromance from Hell

"...a great vampire squid wrapped around the face of humanity, relentlessly jamming its blood funnel into anything that smells like money." *- Matt Taibbi, Rolling Stone investigative journalist describing Goldman Sachs*

The Government sets the boundaries within which the free market is allowed to operate. It is not one versus the other. The boundaries are then blurred when activities and practices that were previously illegal are suddenly now legit. There are also those who start in finance, jump to government to open the cash register drawer further, then jump back to finance making blood money while laughing all the way to the bank.

Robert Rubin started as a lawyer, spent 26 years at Goldman Sachs (even becoming a member of its board and chairman), was Bill Clinton's Secretary of the Treasury from 1995 to 1999, and served as chairman of Citigroup. This guy is so far up the financial industry's ass he's able to perform its colonoscopy just by blinking.

Risky and complex instruments including collateralized debt obligations (CDOs), credit swaps, and derivatives were championed by then-Secretary Rubin and he vehemently opposed any regulation of them even though those financial instruments had already created havoc for Proctor & Gamble and reaped disastrous consequences for Orange County, California with its $1.5 billion default and subsequent bankruptcy. Nevertheless, Rubin's former employer, Goldman Sachs, was profiting enormously from those methods so he wasn't about to rock the boat.

During the Clinton administration, Robert Rubin was a lead figure in repealing the Glass-Steagall Act. That series of laws was enacted in the 1930s after the Great Depression and separated commercial and investment banking. The repeal allowed Wall Street firms to gamble with their depositors' money that was held in affiliated commercial banks. Rubin and Clinton brought down another barrier and allowed Wall Street to creep into more financial sectors and roll the dice with more of Americans' hard earned money.

The Head of the Commodity Futures Trading Commission (CTFC), Brooksley Born, circulated a letter urging more regulation of the untamed derivatives market (suggestions in line with a 1994 General Accounting Office report). Rubin and yet another fraud, Alan Greenspan, publicly railed against that proposed regulation in 1997. In 1998 Rubin made the unusual step for a Secretary of the Treasury by denouncing Born and her proposal while urging the CTFC be stripped of its regulatory authority. A PBS Frontline documentary, "The Warning," highlights how the lack of regulation of the derivatives market played a key role in the financial crisis of 2008.

Rubin even contacted an old crony at the U.S. Treasury Department in 2001 and asked if the department could convince bond-rating agencies not to downgrade the corporate debt of Enron. Enron was a debtor of Citigroup, another organization of bloated parasites.

Citibank has become such an enormous lobbyist and even now writes legislation (laws benefitting themselves) for submittal by their Congressional paid-for puppets in power. Citibank paid Rubin $126 million including $33 million in stock options between 1999 and 2009, when he resigned from the position of Senior Counselor at Citigroup. He received the cash throughout the bailout of Citigroup by the U.S. Treasury and American taxpayers. Utterly disgusting.

Greedy bastard Rubin talks out of both sides of his mouth. In a 2009 Newsweek article he described the financial crisis as a combination of market and credit excesses, low interest rates, massive use of complex derivatives, misguided AAA ratings, stagnant median real wages, abusive mortgage practices, and the over-leveraging of financial institutions. Keep in mind, these were all pies he already put his dirty little fingers into. Clinton called Rubin the "greatest secretary of the Treasury since Alexander Hamilton." Hamilton died from injuries resulting in a duel with Aaron Burr. If we ever bring dueling back, I'd like to challenge scumbag Robert Rubin.

In Bill Clinton's book, *My Life*, he staunchly defends Robert Rubin and notes the times Rubin stood up for him at Cabinet meetings during impeachment talks (that had resulted from Clinton's lies in the first place). Of course he stood up for you, Mr. President. You were helping him aid Wall Street in perpetuating the longest ongoing heist of the American people that we've ever known.

The betrayal of the American people by Republican trickle-down economics was added to by the betrayal of Democrat financial insiders padding their own pockets as well. Both parties are in it for themselves and reelection. If you think they have the interests of regular people in mind, you are simply fooling yourself. Just look at the evidence.

Slow Boat to China, Long Road to Ruin

"I believe democracy is our greatest export. At least until China figures out a way to stamp it out of plastic for 3 cents a unit." – *Stephen Colbert*

Since the days of Alexander Hamilton, many leaders have known our nation had to be well-supplied and they totally grasped the fact that manufacturing had to be a solid part of it. After seeing how badly the colonies' army was equipped and how well the British were armed with ammunition and supplies, then Secretary of the Treasury Hamilton vowed to never have his country in a vulnerable position again. America had a dedicated policy of manufacturing our own essential goods and services while ensuring that other manufacturers around the globe that made critical goods operated in alignment with U.S. interests since 1789.

The year 1993 changed all of that. Those in the large

corporation driver seats laid waste to this system when they struck a deal with China.

President Clinton slammed President Bush the Elder's stance on Chinese trade when the two were jockeying for the White House. Clinton was saying whatever it took to get elected because once in office he followed George H.W. Bush's direction and extended Most-Favored-Nation trading partner status to China. Originally Clinton used China's history of violating human rights as a sticking point, but suddenly Clinton's Secretary of State, Warren Christopher, said the rights issues were being resolved and Clinton led everyone to believe it was now amenable and we should also even pave the way for China's entry into the World Trade Organization (WTO).

Most-Favored-Nation status is usually reserved for partners that help us advance our interests, not undermine them. The United States traded with the former Soviet Union during the Cold War, but at least we had the common sense and intelligence to manage the relationship so that we didn't provide them with anything they could use against us. I wish the same could be said with our Chinese relations.

In 2000, Clinton said granting China Permanent Normal Trade Relations (PNTR) was "a great deal for America. He stated, "We do nothing. They have to lower tariffs. They open up telecommunications for investment. They allow us to sell cars made in America in China at much lower tariffs. They allow us to put our own distributorships there. They allow us to put our own parts there. We don't have to transfer technology or do joint manufacturing in China any more. This is a hundred-to-nothing deal for America when it comes to the economic consequences."

Clinton was foolish, harmful, and imprudent... at best.

Either Clinton had a really foggy crystal ball or he was downright full of it because here's what we got out of the deal:

Trade Deficit: Explosion of the deficit since Clinton opened the door further. In the decade after Most-Favored-Nation trading status was granted, the trade deficit with China grew from 83 billion dollars to an out of control balance of 273 billion dollars.

Cars: General Motors now sells more cars in China than they do in the United States. G.M. even closed 13 U.S. plants after filing for bankruptcy, but it opened 15 in China.

Essential Home Products: Not just shoes and textiles anymore, now smartphones, computers, high-tech products, and even research and development come from China.

Jobs: American companies undercut their own nation that provides them the very freedom and the ability to transact business by shipping jobs away from America.

Economy: It used to be soundly based upon making things ourselves. That in turn provided jobs for Americans and the humming economy helped produce manufactured goods. Now, jobs are disappearing from our shores at an unsustainable rate.

Pay Cuts: That type of decrease in pay had not

happened since the 1930s. The job and domestic investment markets have not recovered even though profits have increased, the stock market has reached new highs, inter-corporate cash continues to flow, and corporate money has poured into the banking market.

Blue Chip (supposedly American) companies including Caterpillar, General Electric, John Deere, and big auto makers invest far more in China than they do here. U.S. Banks even lend more capital to China than they do to entities in the United States.

The Federal Reserve (the Fed) is making matters worse. The secretive Federal Open Market Committee (FMOC) is the policy making arm of the Fed. Members are on written committee record as saying that we DON'T have enough imports coming from China and that unions and workers are "slow to adjust." These policymakers want to weaken people's ability to strike and thus allow even more Chinese goods to come here. Keep in mind, these are many of the same workers who had to take lower paying jobs after the recession.

The inmates are running the asylum and continue to provide as much protection to the Chinese as quickly as they possibly can while undercutting our own country and selling our people down the river.

How U.S. – China Trade Works

China operates on a complex policy depending upon economic mercantilism. Mercantilism is a doctrine that says maximizing net exports is the best route to national prosperity. Discounting and dispatching mercantilism has been the cornerstone of modern economics ever since Adam Smith urged to break away from such tactics in 1776. However, China is still using the policy and we're falling for it hook, line, and sinker.

China rigs its own currency and tax codes to lure businesses and foreign investment away from other countries in a planned and deliberate strategy to change how money flows around the globe. Other countries and nations have done it, but not remotely to the extent we see with China.

China uses predatory pricing when it sets prices below cost to gain market share. Why would a producer willingly take a loss on every sale for a period of time? Once the competition is forced out of the picture because they simply cannot compete with the artificially lower prices the predator simply inflates their prices to above break-even again, thereby profiting because there is no longer another rival who can offer true competition.

Undercutting prices and then jacking them up after the competition is damaged or goes out of business is also a tactic used by Walmart in crowding out mom-and-pop enterprises and other small businesses. If Walmart was a country, it would rank as China's 8th largest trading partner. Corporations or countries: it doesn't matter when they're out making a buck and bleeding their own people dry.

Rampant intellectual property theft by China is also rising. As serious as that is, it's small potatoes compared to the thievery from forced technology transfer, tax policies, and border-adjustable value-added taxes that subsidize exports. Perhaps the biggest and certainly one of the most perverse practices is China's currency manipulation.

Between 1992 and 1994 China led other Asian nations and devalued its currency by a whopping 60%. This made the goods produced in China essentially on sale at a 60% discount. American-made goods looked extremely expensive due to China's deliberately deceptive practices, but what did American corporations and banks do? Well of course they went crazy with investing over there and sending our jobs overseas chasing after money at the expense of our reinvesting in our citizens.

The enormous trade deficit problem is worsened by China's subsidization of American consumerism while at the same time limiting their own. China's runaway mercantilist policies violate the spirit of fair trade markets and tread all over international trade laws. President Obama's dramatic push for the ratification of the Trans Pacific Partnership (TPP) is shrouded in secrecy, but those who have seen limited leaked information apparently say it will make matters even worse. There has been a long line of politicians selling the nation out to China and it needs to be reined in. We need to demand more transparency about the TPP and other proposed agreements.

Taxes, Tariffs, and "Free Trade"

The artificial price disparity between Chinese products and American goods is enlarged by huge differences in taxes and tariffs. When someone in China buys a product from the U.S.A. the Chinese government slaps a 25% tax on it. However, when a consumer in the United States buys a Chinese product it is taxed at only 2.5%. Our government only collects one-tenth on imports than our trading counterparts.

Politicians have allowed this to happen in the name of "free trade."

Some retailers in our country have even purchased American flags from China all the while claiming how patriotic and caring they are about our country. Our jobs apparently aren't as important to them as padding their bottom line.

China has been participating in a trade war and our so-called leaders have given them the keys to the kingdom while escorting them to massive profits. Politicians love to run around screaming "but it's the free market" until they're blue in the face, but they don't seem to understand the free market is established by the boundaries set by the government. All sectors should be working toward common goals instead of selling the future away.

Taxpayers get to foot the bill when "too big to fail" automakers, royally screw up and prove they can't manage a banana stand let alone an automobile manufacturing company. The government bails them out, the cost is passed along to everyone else, and those automakers are allowed to continue shipping jobs away and buying imported parts. It's a vicious cycle and it continues as the government not only guarantees that big businesses won't fail, but those guarantees in turn boost bank credit ratings. Those ratings allow banks to look safer and more stable while at the same time they're still making bad loans and straight up gambling and losing on risky bets with our money. When will it end?

Apple is another serious offender. They get points for originality in product design and marketing, but when netting has to be installed at their Foxconn "factories" to stop suicidal workers from hitting the ground after jumping off roofs, there's a serious issue. The issue apparently isn't a big concern for Apple as they won't improve working conditions or move jobs back to the United States even though they recently made record quarterly profits... again.

Exactly like our stock market, trade with China is a rigged game and we are not winning. There is no equal footing where each nation can make just, fair, and equitable advancement. Steal from the poor, give to the rich, and give the money away: that has been our politicians' answer. Crime apparently does pay.

If everything I've told you so far doesn't make you sick, then the following should put you over the edge: China is the largest holder of American debt. Not only do they have our jobs, they also thrive and grow at our expense at every turn.

Whatever the hell is going on in Washington sure hasn't produced a sustainable strategy. Bought, sold, and paid for politicians have sold us out and shipped America over on a slow boat to China that is quickly gaining speed. We are on a long road to ruin and it's time to make a change of direction.

An important aspect to always remember is that China is not doing these things in a vacuum. It is not "all China's fault." Our elected officials are bending over backwards to allow them to not only get away with it, but they also continue to encourage them to do it through horrible trade practices. Both Republicans and Democrats are not grasping the concept that China is playing the trade game for the long haul. Politicians only think with a short term mentality, saying "free-trade this" and "free-trade that" when they know damn well trade is anything but free. If China was interested in free trade they would be practicing it. The only freedom existing in the version of the game we're playing is being granted to those running the rigged competition. They get even more leeway to manipulate the system and bend the rules in their favor.

Japan once had a very similar economic theory to China's. They too relied on mercantilism and then used rampant currency manipulation. In 1985 President Reagan reached an agreement with France, West Germany, Japan, and the United Kingdom that changed the value of the yen against the dollar by 50%. Similar approaches like Reagan's combined with an increase in tariffs on Chinese goods coming into America can help us fight back.

President Nixon was able to get across-the-board surcharges on Japanese goods imported by the United States in 1971. Japan negotiated a new trading rate with us four months later. China needs our repayments of debt. We have leverage and we should use it.

China blatantly ignores safety and environmental standards. They don't care about the quality of life and will pollute while manufacturing subpar products like defective steel and below-grade drywall. These defective products create problems down the line ranging from structural deficiencies to the cost of labor needed to repair and/or replace those deficiencies. You get what you pay for, and what you pay for often has hidden costs. "Cheapest" can lead to "most expensive" over time.

There is a cycle that is breaking our country:

1) The rich get richer (the Chinese rich get richer as well)
2) Both the poor and middle classes buy cheaper Chinese goods because their household and personal budgets are shrinking
3) Companies ship jobs overseas because they can pay workers less there
4) Those companies make record profits
5) The money from record profits is not reinvested in the United States
6) Banks extend credit, thereby making it

easier to buy Chinese goods

7) Bought-and-paid-for politicians support the banks

8) The United States "prints" more money thus dropping the value of the dollar worldwide

9) A dropping value of the dollar drives up the price that other countries would have to pay to buy our goods

10) U.S. employment suffers because other countries don't buy our products

11) Most of the U.S. suffers economically except for the wealthiest

12) Rinse, repeat.

You would think we would want to break this cycle, but instead our government rewards the biggest perpetrators.

D.C. and G.E.: A Love Affair

Corporate welfare is real and one glaring example is General Electric. They spent $159 million on lobbying efforts from 2007 through 2012. During that same time period they received $19.6 billion from taxpayers in federal support. That's a negative 9 percent tax rate.

What was the result of this continued screwing of taxpayers? In the 4th quarter of 2013 alone, they made $5.4 billion in earnings from operations (around a 20%

increase from the same time in 2012.)

G.E. is out of bounds given their history of increasing top executive pay while laying off substantial portions of rank and file workers. This, of course, is nothing new for the tax dodging corporation. In the 1980s and 1990s, CEO Jack Welch laid off more than 100,000 employees. What was his reward? A golden parachute of over $400 million. Their current batch of executives hasn't fallen far from that diseased tree. Greed and irresponsibility run rampant in their culture. Un-American businesses like G.E. are moochers riding off the backs of the middle class and less fortunate. There is no legitimate reason why taxpayer money should support these corporate welfare-collecting deadbeats.

G.E. also ships jobs and manufacturing to China. Starting in 2007 they outsourced the production of next-generation light bulbs there. G.E. even profits by licensing them their patents while leaving the actual manufacturing outside of U.S. borders.

Proposed Solutions

There is no way that anyone can pretend they have a perfect solution. The strategies I propose are important steps in the direction away from our destructive economic and financial path. Economics, finance, and international trade are complex and the problems around them are many, yet there are things we can do to start unraveling the mess.

I mentioned the Banking Act of 1933 (known as Glass-Steagall) in the section about Robert Rubin. It was intended to forestall bank runs and to help prevent future crises. Not only did it create the Federal Deposit Insurance Corporation (FDIC) but it also puts rules in place which stopped financial institutions from using banking money for speculative investment. From 1933 all the way to the 1990s, if a bank took deposits it could not trade in anything but government bonds and if it engaged in securities it could not make deposits. The partition was lowered further through the Gramm-Leach-Bliley Act, and the anemic Volcker Rule does nothing to stem the tide. I support full re-implementation of Glass-Steagall provisions.

Wall Street banks need to be capped and broken up. Even the most conservative branch of the Fed (Dallas branch) recommends it because they saw the savings and loan crisis originate in Texas during the 1980s.

I discussed in the section about campaign finance that we must get the money out of politics. Supreme Court Justice Nominees who favor repealing Citizens United should be sought as the age of the current bench is fairly high. I also support a Constitutional amendment taking unlimited private money out of public politics and campaigns.

The minimum wage needs to go to at least $15 an hour. Low-income wage earners simply cannot live on current levels which have not been raised in line with inflation. Being able to live and actually have money to spend raises productivity and sets the stage perfectly to propel small businesses. People can only spend money when they have it.

We cannot hold on to the romantic notion that jobs from overseas will suddenly come back. The companies that sell the country out are under no obligation to change as their stockholders are liking what they're seeing. We must adopt a long-term focus as we cannot continue to sacrifice the future for short-term financial gain like current politicians are doing. We have the most potential of any nation on Earth, so we should invest in education and teaching skills in order to create the most economically valuable workforce of today and for the future.

Congress has the power to officially and formally declare other countries currency manipulators and impose sanctions. While it would not be the first move, we need to consider this an option.

Republicans certainly hate them and Democrats have even unfairly turned their backs away from them, but the parties don't realize the need to protect the rights of workers has been and always will be around, and unions are needed. International Monetary Fund (IMF) economists Florence Jaumotte and Carolina Osorio Buitron noted in March 2015 reports that, "Historically, unions have played an important role in the introduction of fundamental social and labor rights [and that] the weakening of unions can lead to less redistribution and higher net income inequality." Like many other expert economists, they called for a "reaffirmation of labor standards that allow willing workers to bargain collectively."

I support updating existing labor laws to make it easier for workers to organize. Real sanctions and fines need to result against employers who illegally fire workers for organizing. High labor standards should be the norm in American trade policy and not an afterthought. Workers' rights will also require better defense and organizational proactivity at the state level. Stronger unions and organized labor will help lessen the inequality crisis and I fully support their rights and agree they need to be recognized and expanded.

CEOs who keep international trade rigged need to be exposed. They're raking in profits at the expense of the entire country. Call them on the carpet and prosecute them when warranted. No one violating these laws should be "too big to jail."

The financial industry needs to be put back in its place. I do not support giving corporate welfare to those firms. If they want to live by the market, they must be ready to die by it.

Those with the most wealth will have to contribute more revenue. They use more. I don't advocate returning to that level, but during the Eisenhower administration the top marginal tax rate (MTR) was 92 percent. I support at least a 2% surtax on the wealth of the richest one-half of one percent. That would bring over $750 billion in revenue over a decade. After all, 95% of all gains in the U.S. between 2009 and 2012 went to the top 1 percent. Executive pay over $1 million should not be tax deductible for corporations as it is now.

Even if we don't use the surtax method, the top marginal tax rates must rise. A system where the top 1% has a highest marginal tax rate of 55% (remember, this is before any tax deductions), the top 2% had a 50% MTR, and the top 5% had 40-45% MTRs would raise over $600 billion in revenue. Economic booms occurred after Reagan's 1982 tax increase and after Clinton's increase in 1993. A middle class with money will make it happen again. The economy will be strengthened when we have upward mobility instead of the current situation of middle class families with even two wage-earners working harder and harder over longer hours to go nowhere.

The rise of Middle-Out Economics takes us away from disaster capitalism and the package of myths promoting supply-side theories. Seventy percent of the U.S. economy is consumer spending and most of that spending is done by the middle class. Increased consumer demand and purchasing power drives real and solid economic growth and profits while allowing responsible capitalism to flourish and the overall standard of living to rise.

6   FIREARMS

Many different foundations, groups, and organizations have conducted a great deal of research regarding gun violence. The only certainty is a lack of rhyme or reason from study to study. I believe the lack of consistency is in part due to bias by those who are paid for conducting some of the studies as well as the vastly different population densities throughout America.

The gun control debate occurring in our current state of political affairs invariably reaches two outcomes: If the Republicans control Congress, they will try everything to boost gun sales and if Democrats are in control they will push for at least some type of partial ban. The result is a political pendulum swinging back and forth depending upon which horrible partisan goons are in charge for the time being. Nothing truly gets accomplished and gun violence has not decreased enough over the long term.

Therefore, I propose that we focus our time, money, and efforts on solving the underlying problem of gun violence in the first place: mental illness.

It's a tough road and critics are obviously correct when they say it is not that easy. The fact is that most of the problems we face are not simple and gun violence is certainly not a quick fix either. Politicians who only seem to focus on short term sound bites are eager to try and push one way or another while they completely ignore the root cause of the issue. Pertaining to gun violence, the underlying evidence is that most sane and responsible people don't grab a weapon of any kind and take innocent lives.

If we attack violent mental illness and allow those afflicted access to mental health care while breaking down societal stigmas about it we will start to address the actual problem.

This goes against the typical responses of both parties. Remember that neither of their approaches have worked. It is time for more in-depth critical thinking and analysis than the usual Republican response of, "Guns are the best things since sliced bread" or the Democrats saying, "We don't think you don't need that specific type of gun." Like most issues, the middle ground is where the majority of people are and it has to be somewhere between the right-wing "let's even sell the things in vending machines" attitude and the left-wing "there's no such thing as a good gun" mentality. By stepping away from this argument and instead focusing on the mental health aspect for the time being lends to helping other areas and people in society as well as directly addressing the origin that underlies violence in the first place. Not only will those in need be able to get help, but we will have a chance at creating a positive spillover effect into other parts of our population.

Half of homeless veterans suffer from some form of mental illness and 70% have substance abuse problems, according to the National Coalition for Homeless Veterans. By focusing collective efforts in a nonpartisan manner to address public mental illness, the government will invariably help homeless veterans in the process. By focusing on a deeper issue we would be able to start addressing the needs of diverse populations and the societal crossover effect to other issues is undeniable.

There is no group, race, or sex that is immune to societal pressures or immune to possible mental illness. Anyone is susceptible. The more people we can aim to help the broader the likely impact of the resulting benefits to individuals, families, and society as a whole.

Mentalhealth.gov reports one in five American adults experienced a mental health issue in 2011. They also state one of every ten young people experience a period of major depression. The Federal Substance Abuse and Mental Health Services Administration reports that 9.6 million adults are reported to have some type of mental illness. Many states are dropping the ball with not expanding Medicaid, Florida being one of them. Focusing on access to mental health care is imperative.

The results of every political gun debate are already predetermined. We need a different strategy or else we just get more of the same. By tackling the cause instead of the effect, we will also preserve the rights inherent in the Second Amendment.

We could argue forever about interpretation of the laws and rulings concerning our right to bear arms, but at the end of the day, that argument does little to curtail actual gun violence. The fact remains that courts have upheld our citizens' right to have guns. Some can disagree all they want, but of all the arguments made and all the time and money spent, what has that accomplished to even slow gun violence? Not enough.

We can therefore accept that we have to redefine the parameters of the questions regarding efforts to lessen gun violence. I believe we should reframe the bulk of the debate from "Do we have the right?" (because that question has never addressed the root cause) to, "What can be done while still preserving our rights as we currently believe those rights to be?"

The banning of firearms erodes our liberties. At what point will those in power draw the line? After all, this is our Second Amendment. We need to protect this right.

The rights of gun owners can also be protected without acting like careless jackasses. Republicans need to act responsibly and not like Mitch McConnell when he waved a rifle around over his head at CPAC. It's a bad symbolic idea after yet another string of school shootings. Actions like that are not helping the situation, adding anything of substance, and are exercises in foolishness. Don't add fuel to the fire or use scare tactics to drum up gun sales for your firearm industry lobbyists who give you campaign money. The NRA's Wayne LaPierre also needs to tone down the "absolutely batshit crazy" factor a bunch. To say the least, it's irresponsible to send mixed messages.

I believe we must protect firearm rights. I would not support any type of specific gun ban because any discussion in that direction takes resources away from combatting the true root cause of gun violence. We should change our focus from participating in the gun debate's predetermined outcome of making no progress to taking a different approach that will reduce gun violence, produce benefits to a wide part of society, and protect our Second Amendment rights.

7   IMMIGRATION

Congress has yet again failed to produce immigration reform so President Obama has recently tried to use Executive powers in an attempt to wake the Legislative Branch up.

Deferred Action for Childhood Arrivals (DACA) allows certain undocumented immigrants who entered the United States prior to turning 16 years old and before June 2007 to receive a renewable two-year work permit and exemption from deportation. It does not give legal status or provide a path to citizenship and it was started by the Obama administration in June 2012. Even Mitt Romney stated that he would honor the grants of deferred action approved under DACA until more permanent legislation was put into place. There are currently a few bottlenecks, but expansion is planned and I view it as a patch. Additional aspects need to be addressed as neither DAPA (Deferred Action for Parental Accountability) nor DACA is a long-term solution. Temporarily speaking, keeping President Obama's policies in place for the time being adds to our national gross domestic product according to the Hoover Institution.

Congress has to act even if DACA and DAPA don't stand the test of time. At the time of this writing, those actions are being legally challenged. No matter the outcome, it is undeniable that Congress has the full power to address the problem and if the actions were beyond the scope of the Executive Branch then Congress should immediately move to replace them in kind at very least temporarily so there is no drop off. We need long-term progress with consistency as we build the bridge to more permanent solutions.

Federal reports show that Florida and the rest of the nation will substantially benefit economically from immigration reform. We must protect our borders while allowing law-abiding immigrants to work here through a regulated system. Improvements in immigration policy will also help rekindle our nation's commitment to provide opportunity for everyone.

U.S. Secretary of Agriculture Tom Vilsack released a report estimating immigration reform would increase Florida families' total income by $6.5 billion within seven years and that the creation of worker programs, combined with a process to earn citizenship, would also create more than 22,000 jobs statewide.

Approximately 25% of Florida's workforce is foreign-born and nearly 30% of our state's business owners are immigrants.

Let's look at immigration's impact in one economic area: agriculture. If we removed immigrant labor from agriculture statewide it would cause between $560.4 million and $1.01 billion in short-term agricultural production losses alone. Florida's agricultural industry generates over $104 billion in revenue each year.

There are many complex issues and moving parts in the search for solutions, however there is one area that people can make a change in instantly. Screaming and yelling at immigrant children as they are being processed and transported at the border is pretty low. Why would someone wave signs and shout obscenities to these small kids often sent to travel across strange lands alone? They're children. The protestors are completely entitled to their views and opinions and by all means can voice them in the appropriate forums. All I am saying is a little empathy for already scared little kids would go a long way.

Sean Patrick Guthrie

8   THE MILITARY VS. THE MILITARY-INDUSTRIAL COMPLEX

To me, the military has been and always will be about the people in it. Crooked and misguided politicians use the military as a pawn and they have sold its people out to the military-industrial complex. The military and the military-industrial complex are NOT the same.

The military is comprised of our soldiers, our fighters, and those who provide them support. The military-industrial complex concerns the money and the policy relationship between legislators, the military, and the arms industry.

The military is made up of the families and loved ones of those who serve. The military-industrial complex cranks out surplus and then sells it to police departments, border patrols, and independent security organizations to make even more profit riding on original taxpayer funding.

The military is made out of our heroes. The military-industrial complex is comprised of a series of corporations "competing" for no-bid contracts.

We have a military capability ranging the entire spectrum of being as precise as delivering death up someone's urethra from thousands of miles away with the push of a button in a control room all the way up to obliterating the world and potentially all life on it with mass nuclear weapon use. What the political clowns in Washington willfully ignore for the sake of money and personal profit above all else is the fact that we already have the capability, but the actual people make the military and those people need more help than they are currently receiving.

We need to take part of the funding that is in our bloated defense budget and actually help the military, the people, instead of buying more equipment to put into surplus or purchasing additional aircraft carriers even the Pentagon says they don't need or want, just to appease lobbyists. Contractors want to maximize return to shareholders at any cost for financial gain and don't have our defense or the people providing the defense as their top priority.

Our national defense will not suffer if we provide health care for our veterans nor will our national defense suffer if we help all veterans in need to seek and obtain mental health assistance. If we can find endless money for veteran-creating war, we can find the money to take care of the people who fight in it.

Congress doesn't do anything to show they care or appreciate the fact that these are the people who sacrificed for this country. Their response is to send more generations to fight their manufactured political wars. Congress owes them, and the time to take care of those who took care of us is long overdue. The rolling war machine driven by politicians and their bankrollers is responsible and should share blame and embarrassing shame for the failure to provide even basic care for many military veterans. What the hell is wrong with those people? The blood of every homeless, hungry, and uncared for soldier on the streets is on your hands because of inaction, ineptitude, and not caring enough about their well-being.

Some politicians claim they "support the military" then commit money away from the actual people who served. They spend national revenue on what our commanders don't even want. They throw our tax dollars into the vast behemoth referred to as the military-industrial complex.

In 1961 President Dwight D. Eisenhower addressed his growing concern about the military-industrial complex in his final message to the nation during his farewell address. To put it in context, that was a much different time. Back then, ex-Presidents faded into obscurity after leaving office and didn't do press tours or interviews like they do now. He found it so crucial to warn the American people of the growing threat that he used his last chance to speak to Americans as their

Commander-In-Chief to denounce the military-industrial complex. Keep in mind, this is someone who fought and led through both world wars, and that includes being Commander of the Allied Forces in Europe during WWII. President Eisenhower stated:

"A vital element in keeping the peace is our military establishment. Our arms must be mighty, ready for instant action, so that no potential aggressor may be tempted to risk his own destruction.

"Until the latest of our world conflicts, the United States had no armaments industry.

"This conjunction of an immense military establishment and a large arms industry is new in the American experience. The total influence-economic, political, even spiritual- is felt in every city, every State house, (and) every office in the federal government. We recognize the imperative need for this development. Yet we must not fail to comprehend its grave implications. Our toil, our resources and livelihood are all involved; so is the very structure of our society.

"In the councils of government, we must guard against the acquisition of unwarranted influence, whether sought or unsought, by the military-industrial complex. The potential for the disastrous rise of misplaced power exists and will persist.

"We must never let the weight of this combination endanger our liberties or democratic processes. We should take nothing for granted. Only an alert and knowledgeable citizenry can compel the proper meshing of the huge industrial and military machinery of defense with our peaceful methods and goals, so that security and liberty can prosper together."

We must listen to President Eisenhower's warning and realize the situation we are facing. Politicians feed arms manufacturers and contractors while padding their own pockets and campaign spending accounts. These same politicians are the ones urging military involvement at every turn. They operate on the notion that there is a lot of money to be made in solving a problem, but there's oh so much more to be made by prolonging problems and creating new ones. We have the largest defense budget in the history of the world, yet we have so many who have served not getting even the most basic care and respect they need. The military contracting sector has become known for overdue and over budget projects and the "jobs program" portion of this necessary, yet bloated industry is outpacing the increase in efficiency we require for defense. Our priorities are out of whack and we need to flip them for the military's sake.

Sean Patrick Guthrie

9   SOCIAL EQUALITY

Equal Pay

The gender pay gap is still a large issue in workplaces. Research shows the median hourly wage for women was 84% that of men during 2012 compared to 64% in 1980. However, the wage gap is not decreasing as quickly as some claim. The division hardly moved in the past decade and the difference even expanded from 2005 to 2008 and from 2011 to 2012.

Harvard economist, Claudia Godin says the gap is not related to having less women in higher-paying fields because even female financial specialists make 66 percent of what their male counterparts make, female doctors earn 71 percent, and female lawyers and judges make 82 percent. That's all controlling for age, race, hours and education.   Gender discrimination accounts for 25 to 40 percent of the pay gap depending on which economic report you look at. Employers must be more transparent about compensation. To accelerate the closing of the pay gap employers can also stop rewarding JUST long hours and being available around the clock and instead reward high-quality work while giving employees the flexibility to deal with life's events, thereby bringing more natural balance. Family-friendly policies boost morale and productivity.

Around 2/3 of U.S. children have both or their only parent working full-time. How do they do it? Parents are stretched entirely too thin. Congress needs to pass some family leave bills as their action in this area is seriously overdue.

Allowing more unionization has also been shown to narrow the difference. Raising the minimum wage will help women as 2/3 of workers making the minimum are female. We should also pursue desegregating the workforce by removing any potential barriers to allowing qualified women to pursue careers in historically male-heavy industries like manufacturing.

Outside of government, private firms can work internally to detect if there is a gender bias and if so to get it in line. Pay increases or bonuses should be based on annually established goals for threshold, target and maximum.

The World Economic Forum released a report in 2014 stating we may not see gender pay equality until 2095. We can take time off of that estimate by using some of the strategies described above.

Marriage

I'm divorced, but if my ex-wife and I were around prior to 1967 we may have had problems getting married in the first place. Prior to that, interracial marriage was not fully legalized. My parents' backgrounds are white, but her mother's side is white and her father's side is black. Courts have decided that it is a violation of civil liberties to deny marriage based on race.

The same framing of civil rights infringement can also be applied to same-sex marriage. Civil liberties are under attack and discrimination is rampant. Marriage between consenting people of age should not be defined rigidly, therefore implying one sexual preference is superior to another. Equal rights should be available to all.

Racism and homophobia are simply forms of bigotry. It's time to wake up and realize we are all existing on this single planet together. To me, it underscores our responsibility to deal more kindly with one another while we realize the full and equal Constitutional rights of all Americans.

Race

My Mom, JFK, and Star Trek: perhaps an odd combination at first glance, but I promise it will make sense by the end of this section. I am incredibly thankful I was educated about race at a very early age and those three influences played significant roles in forming my basic feelings about racial equality. Like many, I learned such a tremendous amount from my Mom. I have memories from around age 5 of her stressing that people are pretty much the same regardless of race. It's a lesson she would reinforce throughout my childhood and beyond.

Around that age, I would sometimes look through a coffee table book my Mom had about the JFK presidency. A few parts dealt with racial relations and what JFK and RFK were doing about the situation. I don't recall the book exactly, but I do remember the overall tone of it and especially that section as being extremely positive and hopeful of racial equality in the future. I was a wee little lad back then, so I assumed by the time I was an adult that things would be a lot better. Of course we know what the situation is currently, but that vision of a future with racial equality has really remained and inspired me from my early childhood on.

My assessments about racial division were further reinforced by my sister, Tricia, who was nineteen years older than me (she has since passed). She and I would watch Star Trek reruns and she would explain things if the plot was over my head because I was a kid. It is widely known that the show boldly covered a great deal of moral ground, ethical dilemmas, and pertinent issues and that the series broke new social ground especially when it originally ran in the 1960s. Some episodes dealt with race and one even featured the first interracial kiss on television. I became aware at a young age that racism is foolish, contributes nothing to society, and is just plain wrong. I am deeply grateful I overcome the racial bias plaguing many of those around us.

I could go on for quite a long time about the many moral wrongs and violations of civil rights that are still ongoing and many important conversations obviously needs to take place as soon as possible, but for the time being I am going to limit the scope of the following section to what the federal government can do to broaden access to allow participation in the most fundamental levels of our democracy. How can one feel any sense of equality or part in society if they are not allowed to be a part of it from the beginning?

Voting is the most powerful non-violent weapon in a true democracy. The ability to vote is at the core of our nation and minority voters across the country are not being given that ability. We can't even get our act together with voting in U.S. territories as they're caught up in political games too.

Gerrymandering needs to end. All citizens should have equal representation under the law and not according to manufactured partisan geography. Equal voting representation needs to be established by dismantling and replacing district lines. Access to voting should be available for all who wish to do it and should not be hindered in any way, especially by a party attempting to influence elections.

In America, we should be celebrating our democracy and doing everything possible to make it easier for people to participate in the political process. Election Day should be a national holiday so that everyone has the time and opportunity to vote and make their voices heard through the most powerful non-violent exercising of rights we have. While this would not be a cure-all, it would indicate a national commitment to create a more vibrant democracy.

Racism is constantly ongoing even though the Supreme Court and Congress think that it's dead. To see the Voting Rights Act as some kind of quaint relic or to think it is no longer needed or valuable in today's society is to deny even the very basic undercurrents of recent events. The skillfully organized assault on voting rights in recent years is unlike anything Americans have seen since the Jim Crow era, making it critically important to bring the full power of the Voting Rights Act back.

It is blatantly obvious there is a lot of work to be done, but these are just a few areas the government has the direct power to address in the short term.

Women

I believe in full equality under the law and equality of opportunity for all women. I also believe a woman's actions regarding reproductive health (from education to preventative services to abortion) are protected civil liberties.

Overreaching laws are dictating medical decisions

instead of doctors and patients. Access to essential reproductive (and other) health care should be expanded and we should not stand for the artificial limits of liberty imposed, including those that disproportionately and harshly treat low-income, minority, and immigrant women. Legal, safe, and affordable contraception should be available. Abortion rights need to be legally upheld as well.

Access to health care is also an economic issue. A woman should be able to control her own health and reproductive rights because her health and choices make a very real and lasting impact on not only her financial stability and survival, but also on her family.

Women should have uncensored information and the power needed to make their own decisions outside of intrusive government interference.

10   SOCIAL SECURITY

The Social Security program attempts to provide financial security for citizens over certain ages, qualifying disabled Americans, their families, and their survivors. With the average yearly benefit only $15,120, we must guard against cuts to ensure millions who paid into the system actually get what is promised to them. I support expanding Social Security benefits and I vigorously oppose any cut or decrease in benefits. According to the actual numbers and hard data, the Social Security system is solvent.

Every election brings out those who resort to fear mongering claims that Social Security is going to implode in the near future. With ads and claims flying around like a swarm of rabid bats it may be easy to momentarily believe some of the lies, however careful analysis shoots holes in the criticism and shines light on the facts.

FACT: Social Security has NOT contributed to federal deficit growth.

Social Security has never contributed a single cent to any deficit in the over 75 years it has existed. Social Security is sustained by a dedicated payroll tax that fully funds the program separate and distinct from annual discretionary budgets. When politicians spew only sound bites of information they may mention a, "Social Security deficit," but that refers to the area of ingoing-outgoing payment flows and not to the federal deficit as they are quite simply unrelated. It's an apples and oranges type of comparison designed only to confuse people.

FACT: Social Security is structurally sound.

When insane Texan Rick Perry called Social Security a Ponzi scheme he implied it is an inherently unsustainable system and destined to collapse. He's grossly incorrect as usual because Social Security and pyramid schemes differ dramatically. The Social Security system never runs out of new enrollees to sustain itself because people continue to have children and those children become workers who pay into the Social Security system and trust fund. Ponzi and pyramid schemes are notorious for hiding where the actual money goes. However, Social Security has a lengthy and detailed funding and payment paper trail. Adjustments along the way are needed as population figures are dynamic, but the system is inherently sound as new generations enter the system.

FACT: The private sector controlling Social Security would be disastrous.

Permitting the private sector to gamble with retirement is not a good idea at all. The tradeoff of potential reward versus the risk is staggering. The number one commandment of risk management is to never risk more than you are willing to lose. Financial institutions gamble with funds constantly and often lose significant portions of capital and have potential to lose absolutely everything they risked to start with. What makes you think they would be cautious with your retirement money? They love to bet on equity investments, which do show a historic higher rate of return but bear significantly more risk. Do you want Wall Street rolling the dice with your retirement money any more than they already do? If you do, go over to the nearest casino and press your luck because you'll get better odds because unlike Wall Street's gambling, at least casinos are somewhat regulated.

FACT: Social Security is solvent.

Let us examine what would happen if ABSOLUTELY NOTHING is done to Social Security. Stressing the point again, we're operating on the premise that ABSOLUTELY NOTHING is changed. The Social Security trust fund will still be able to pay benefits at the current level until 2033 to 2037. At that point, EVEN WITHOUT MODIFICATION, revenues will be able to pay out 75% of promised benefits.

FACT: Even if the government does nothing we would be relatively okay for a time.

Even if the federal government did absolutely nothing over the next decades to alter Social Security, a one-time cut of 25% in 2033 would make the program solvent into the foreseeable future. Of course that would not be an optimal tactic as there are numerous alternative strategies, however, it underscores just how solid the Social Security system is indeed. Even at 1.9 workers per retiree in 2038, 81% of the current, inflation-adjusted rate would be paid out without increasing revenue at all. These facts obliterate any scare tactics politicians routinely use.

FACT: The Social Security Administration help line is NOT the best place for information.

They actually put the newest and least trained people on the phones. Whenever I called them during my time as a financial advisor, it turned out I knew more about the system than the representative on the line did, even about readily available and published information. I urge the Social Security Administration to put qualified people on the phone banks because accurate information is necessary for people needing service. How and when recipients file makes an enormous impact on the amount of benefit they will receive for the rest of their lives and the lives of their survivors. Get your act together Social Security Administration decision makers.

Sean Patrick Guthrie

11   ONWARD

New Power

Jeremy Heimans boldly examines the future of politics and activism in his brilliant TED Talk, "What New Power Looks Like." He speaks about Anna Hazare, a 77 year old anticorruption and social activist on the digital cutting edge. As in the United States, elites in India ignore corruption. In 2011 Hazare ran an enormous campaign using traditional non-violent means, but soon realized a hunger strike would not be enough in the 21st century.

Hazare then turned to mobile activism. He first asked people to send him a text message if they supported and believed in his efforts against corruption. He initially received 80,000 responses. Hazare altered his method by asking supporters to leave him a missed call.

Why missed calls? In the global south, missed calls are culturally important as they allow a person to communicate something (running late, miss you, love you, etc.) to another while avoiding the charges associated with sending texts or completing calls.

The result was one of the largest coordinated actions in human history. Thirty-five million people left Anna Hazare missed calls. From that point he actively organized hundreds of thousands in the streets of India to further rally against rampant corruption.

Technology is a means, but it can definitely aid in shifting power back to the people. Power and influence do not have to come from the top down. Old power is increasingly taking a back seat to new power.

New power is the deployment of mass participation and peer coordination to create change and shift outcomes.

I wish to encourage heavy involvement in politics and government by average citizens.

Another example of using new power effectively is Beppe Grillo. Not only an Italian blogger, but with a minimal political structure and only some online tools he won more than 25 percent of the entire Italian national vote in 2013.

Airbnb has radically disrupted the hotel industry without owning a single square foot of real estate.

Kickstarter has raised over 1.5 billion dollars from more than 8 million people for more than 80,000 creative projects. The structure of all of these innovative examples differed wildly from the old power models.

Old power is held like a currency. New power works like a current.

Old power is held by a few. New power is made by many.

Old power is all about download, new power is about information upload and sharing.

More participation and peer coordination are essential in the 21st century. New power is not the inevitable winner as old power invariably pushes back. Tiny companies started in garages can now disrupt entire industries and it is time for average people to get more involved and make themselves heard in the same way. Collectively, our actions will make some noise to change some extremely nasty habits in Washington D.C.

New power operates with a belief that we should have government transparency and the view that the more light there is shining on something, the better. This is in stark contrast to the current method of making comfortable arrangements behind closed doors.

New power values participation and a do-it-yourself approach. It eschews some of the professionalization and specialization that were all the rage in the 20th century. Heimans goes on to say,

> "If you are old power, the most important thing you can do is to occupy yourself before others occupy you, before you are occupied. Imagine that a group of your biggest skeptics are camped in the heart of your organization asking the toughest

questions and they can see everything inside of your organization. And ask them, would they like what they see and should our model change?"

Consolidation and action is needed for new power to grow. Public goods problems would benefit enormously from mass participation and peer coordination. When democracy flourishes it empowers people and changes the way they feel about their own agency and abilities. It not only changes the way we relate to authority and institutions, but also how we relate to each other.

I urge people of every age and especially young people to get involved civically, politically, and in the community.   Think critically and recognize the importance of dialogue with people regardless of whether or not they are on the other side of an ideological divide. In the big picture of things there are often more similarities than differences between ourselves and others. Finding common ground is vital to communicating effectively.

Some in previous generations have failed us unintentionally and some have planned it for their own benefit while essentially forsaking the future. We must take a new approach to solve the problems facing us all. Many of our problems are man-made and therefore can be solved by man. We must elect leaders who analyze to the past to learn from mistakes, but who also look to the future to see how we can use our amazing potential.

Both parties just don't do that and are detached from normal people and the level of that detachment is at an all-time high. Politicians cannot see our potential from their ivory towers.

Independent candidates must embrace new power methodologies if we are to end the reign of bought-and-paid-for politicians. We regular people must use new power and creative ways to defeat big money politics. I have plenty of effective, extremely low-cost plans which will roll out as the campaign unfolds and I look forward to sharing them with you.

How I'm a Different Breed

Working within the institution without being institutionalized is vitally important. With no term limits in Congress, we have been overrun with career politicians doing nothing but growing more and more removed from the problems facing average Americans. These fixtures in the government machine become increasingly out of touch with each passing decade they spend planted in office legislating ineffectively.

I promise to be different from them yet again. I will only serve two terms. I believe that is long enough to make a positive impact, but short enough to allow others to lead and participate in our legislative process in that position as well.

Legislators in major parties are expected to fundraise and solicit donations for at least an average of four hours daily. Begging for money obviously takes time away from the job they were trusted by the people to perform. My philosophy of using creative and inexpensive methods to communicate and organize negates the often-seen pandering to check-waving oligarchs accustomed to buying votes. If you aren't bought, you can't be sold. Picture a legislator actually using time productively. It's easy to imagine if you try.

Here is yet another way I'm a different breed- I will not have any TV commercials. Those things reside at the junction of annoyance, intrusiveness, and insult, not to mention television advertisements cost enormous sums of money which would be better spent elsewhere. I will not have to raise funds to air those overcooked monstrosities in a medium already grossly played out by politicians, thus in stark contrast to the groveling competition pleading for massive campaign dollars. The more money they take, the more favors they owe. When you see my opponents' commercials, remember I am NOT running ads, NOT wasting money, NOT hijacking your time, NOR am I insulting your intelligence. Campaigns should be campaigns and not full-on marketing blitzes hitting you everywhere you go in normal life so much they become nightmare-fuel.

I will not require money for billboards either. Nature is already blotted out enough as is. After all, who truly desires to look up and see the messages from assorted knuckleheads running for office plastering the sky? Yard signs are also obnoxious and I will not be using them either. My campaign will also save truckloads of money and precious natural resources by being paperless whenever I can.

We need critical thinking abilities more than ever in the 21st century. Part of my creative campaign plan involves my YouTube channel. I will present content through an opt-in fashion instead of the in-your-face tactics the traditional politicians bombard you with incessantly. The show will be produced as inexpensively as possible with an extremely limited budget in order to motivate those out there who don't have massive campaign war chests either. Many surprises await!

Senators John McCain and Lindsey Graham proudly stated they have never even sent an email like that is some type of badge of honor. It's not. It shows their inability and unwillingness to adapt. Unlike the current batch of technologically ignorant legislators, I actually know what it takes to communicate effectively in the 21st century.

Bill Maher sums up our current political system correctly when he says: "... we don't have a left and a right party in this country anymore. We have a center-right party, and a crazy party. Over the last thirty-odd years, Democrats have moved to the right, and the right has moved into a mental hospital. So what we have is one perfectly good party for hedge-fund managers, credit card companies, banks, defense contractors, big agriculture, and the pharmaceutical lobby- that's the Democrats. And they sit across the aisle from a small group of religious fanatics, flat-Earthers, and Civil War reenactors who mostly communicate by AM radio and call themselves the Republicans, and who actually worry that Obama is a socialist. Socialist? He's not even a liberal."

Regardless of alleged political and ideological differences, many Democrats in office simply do not practice what they preach. Part of the party has no backbone and will compromise beliefs at the sight of their own shadows while others are grossly inept in their attempts to adhere to principles. Look at how far they have shifted and how far their party leaders have allowed the party to slide to the right. Democrats also undercut America by taking money from enormous corporations and banks just like their Republican counterparts.

The result is a public still thinking they must pick one side or the other all while being fooled there is any difference in intent. Both parties contain stooges working for their big-money puppeteers. These people only have regard for normal, regular people when election season rears its ugly head, the regard vanishes once an election winner is crowned, and the capacity of the regard revolved only around getting or maintaining their power. They're all in it for those same reasons: gaining and maintaining power and fueling the money machine that's stifling and suffocating America while putting money in their own pockets at the same time. Why does everyone feel like they have to pick a team? The divide and conquer strategy is being played out with brilliance and the public is losing because of it.

It is time for independents and free-thinkers to rise above dual party politics to bring credibility and progress back to our government and to our people.

Differentiation from the status quo is highly encouraged when current circumstances can be so much better, especially in this day and age.

The Big Picture

Critics label me "Progressive" as if it is supposed to be an insult, but being Progressive is simply supporting a return to basics concerning the morals of democracy. I happily do not answer to either party as both parties are horrible and have strayed away from fundamental concepts we all must rely upon in the 21st century.

Democracy requires that citizens care about each other and take both personal and social responsibility to act on that care. I believe the moral mission of government is to protect and empower all citizens equally. We do that by strengthening the public.

The public is the system of resources necessary for a decent private life and for thriving private enterprise. Public resources include education, health care, roads and bridges, police and military, communication, fair justice, clean air, parks, safe food, and much more.

No one makes it on his or her own without the public. The private depends on a strong public. Very large private businesses deliver their goods using public roads. The public police department provides a deterrent to theft and product damage at private warehouses. A private burning manufacturing plant is put out by the publicly-funded fire department.

Employers benefit from a smarter workforce taught through better public education. Large private corporations use public resources to a much larger extent, so they should bear more responsibility in funding the revenue needed to maintain the public.

One of the most important series of questions we must quickly answer concerns the gross level of inequality and the balance between the corporate private and the public. Wealth in and of itself is not a bad thing at all, but we should strive to have wealth without greed. The major problems compound when there is an enormously disproportional concentration of money. Catastrophic threats to liberty exist when that wealth buys political power.

Corporate government dismantles the nation as we know it, love it, and need it to be. Dismantling the public destroys the sanctity and safety of American private life and the basis of most businesses. We need liberty from corporate government.

We can and must return to fair capitalism. Our current system has surpassed the disaster capitalism stage and has gone directly to extortion. Middle class taxpayers are forced to subsidize Wall Street's risky bets and then forced to pay to bail them out. Large private businesses fail from horrible management and taxpayers foot the bill to give them bailout charity money. If you truly want to let laissez-faire economics play out, then you have to live by the free market and die by the free market. Fair capitalism must be based on justice as well as justness in line with corporate profits. We need to end rampant corporate mooching.

Trickle-down economics is the most damaging set of lies ever told and sold. Corporations are not "job creators." Customers are job creators. Without customers, corporations don't exist. Trickle-down economics focuses on supply, but without demand an economic system disintegrates.

Middle-Out economics creates demand by putting more money in the hands of the middle class. Businesses grow as middle-America now has money to spend. My view of a strong American economy is when it functions for the betterment of the nation and all of our citizens by providing the products, goods, and services we need through fair economic competition while being accountable to customers, fully recognizing workers' rights, and providing living wages.

The fights will be many and the work will be hard as we act to preserve our future. More people every day realize we have been led astray by greed and misused power. We can and must bring long lasting benefits for future generations. People are uniting for the common cause of stopping the dual-party system's two-headed monster of bad government and reckless businesses.

I look forward to bringing you more analysis about these issues as well as additional topics. This is just a broad overview and more specifics on my plans will roll out over the next year and a half until the election. You are guaranteed to witness a campaign the likes of which you have never seen before. As always: continue questioning, commit to learning, and keep fighting.

Notes

1   A Brief Background

16   Godin, Seth. *Purple Cow: Transform Your Business by Being Remarkable.* New York: Portfolio, 2003. Print.

17   Note: When I talk about corporations I mean the large, powerful block of often freeloading, tax-dodging, multinational operations and not small businesses, which truly form the backbone of our country.

17   *Small businesses... pay the taxes that the largest corporations avoid:* http://www.huffingtonpost.com/2013/08/08/small-business-taxes_n_3727270.html.

18   *enormous corporations... a leading driver of income inequality:* http://www.washingtonpost.com/opinions/how-america-became-uncompetitive-and-unequal/2014/06/13/a690ad94-ec00-11e3-b98c-72cef4a00499_story.html.

18   *analyzed 1,799 policy issues and found*: http://www.cheatsheet.com/politics/wealthy-americans-run-washington-is-populism-just-a-big-lie.html/?a=viewall.

18   *(corporations and their lobbyists) interests are totally misaligned with the interests of the people and it is demonstrated when those same huge companies threaten to leave every year:* http://www.washingtonpost.com/business/economy/corporate-tax-dodgers-leave-the-rest-of-us-to-foot-the-bill/2014/07/11/de311d1a-06c2-11e4-a0dd-f2b22a257353_story.html.

18   *Governments in other nations bind corporate interests to those of workers and organized labor through legislation:* http://robertreich.org/post/113130324775.

18   *American corporations distribute a smaller share to their workers than European or Canadian companies and American executives make a lot more than those in other wealthy countries:* http://www.nytimes.com/2014/04/23/upshot/the-american-middle-class-is-no-longer-the-worlds-richest.html?_r=0.

19   *the biggest profit margins in 40 years all while rank and file workers in the U.S. receive stagnant wages*: http://www.cheatsheet.com/expert-2/u-s-companies-most-profitable-in-more-than-40-years.html/

19   *put in more hours, receive fewer vacation hours, and are not even guaranteed maternity leave:* http://www.theguardian.com/us-news/2014/dec/03/-sp-america-

only-developed-country-paid-maternity-leave.

19 *secretive Trans Pacific Partnership (TPP):*
http://www.theguardian.com/us-news/2015/may/12/trans-pacific-partnership-explainer

2 Campaign Finance

21 *The result of the 5-4 split decision allows exorbitant sums of cash with no limitation:*
http://www.fec.gov/law/litigation/McCutcheon.shtml.

22 *...$157 billion between 2013 and 2015. $157 billion is more wealth....:*
http://www.motherjones.com/politics/2015/04/bernie-sanders-inequality-president-interview.

3 Education

26 *they're just like little, drunk adults:*
a)   http://www.buzzfeed.com/awesomer/reasons-kids-are-pretty-much-just-tiny-drunk-adults#.ncrrY70J
b)   http://www.huffingtonpost.com/2015/03/17/babies-are-tiny-drunk-adults_n_6887476.html

27-30 *The duties of an efficient education system:*
http://www.ted.com/talks/sir_ken_robinson_bring_on_the_revolution?language=en.

31 *Khan says:* The TED site provides the following synopsis: "Salman Khan talks about how and why he created the remarkable Khan Academy, a carefully structured series of educational videos offering complete curricula in math and, now, other subjects. He shows the power of interactive exercises, and calls for teachers to consider flipping the traditional classroom script — give students video lectures to watch at home, and do 'homework' in the classroom with the teacher available to help."
http://www.ted.com/talks/salman_khan_let_s_use_video_to_reinvent_education?language=en.

33 *The 2009 stimulus package included $7.2 billion:*
http://www.cnet.com/news/stimulus-bill-includes-7-2-billion-for-broadband/

34 *The trend of college prices in the U.S. growing quicker than the rate of inflation has existed since 1972:* "The bad news is that cumulative undergraduate debt is rising as real incomes haven't grown for more than a decade except for top earners, said Sandy Baum and Jennifer

Ma, the (College Board) report authors."
http://www.bloomberg.com/news/articles/2014-11-13/college-tuition-in-the-u-s-again-rises-faster-than-inflation.

34   *education rates have spiraled out of control*:
http://www.economist.com/node/16960438.

34   *President Obama told:*
http://www.ontheissues.org/celeb/barack_obama_education.htm.

34   *The Obama administration is now coming out with a way*:
https://www.whitehouse.gov/the-press-office/2013/08/22/fact-sheet-president-s-plan-make-college-more-affordable-better-bargain-.

35   *Data shows personal earning power*:
http://www.forbes.com/sites/michakaufman/2015/03/20/is-college-still-worth-it/.

35   *$1.2 trillion of student debt exists in America*:
http://college.usatoday.com/2015/04/08/national-student-loan-debt-reaches-a-bonkers-1-2-trillion/.

36   *the 15 largest for-profit education companies received 86% of their revenue from federal aid*:
http://consumerist.com/2015/02/05/should-for-profit-colleges-be-allowed-to-spend-taxpayers-money-to-put-their-names-on-nfl-stadiums/.

36   *the University of Phoenix will spend $154.5 million for the naming rights*: http://sports.espn.go.com/nfl/news/story?id=2603052.

36   *power to address the problem:* http://www.acenet.edu/advocacy-news/Pages/Higher-Education-Act.aspx.

36   *Corinthian University after it was found to have doctored job placement data*: http://www.bloomberg.com/news/articles/2015-04-14/u-s-fines-corinthian-colleges-30-million-for-misrepresentation.

38   *The current interest rates:*
https://studentaid.ed.gov/sa/types/loans/interest-rates#what-are-the-interest-rates-of-federal-student-loans.

38   *Federal Open Market Committee*:
http://www.federalreserve.gov/monetarypolicy/fomc.htm.

38   *the federal funds target rate is only 0% to 0.25%:*
http://www.newyorkfed.org/markets/omo/dmm/fedfundsdata.cfm.

40   *Pearson is a London-based mega-corporation... connections to seedy American Legislative Exchange Council (ALEC)...*: http://www.truth-out.org/news/item/18442-flow-chart-exposes-common-cores-myriad-corporate-connections#.

41   *STEAM teaching systems:* http://steamedu.com/.

42   *In its 2013 report titled, "Talent Shortage Survey Research Results*:
     http://www.manpowergroup.com/wps/wcm/connect/587d2b45-
     c47a-4647-a7c1-
     e7a74f68fb85/2013_Talent_Shortage_Survey_Results_US_high+res.pd
     f?MOD=AJPERES.

4   Our Environment, Animals, and Purple Dog Animal Sanctuary

46   *repeal of solar rebates in 2014*:
     http://ecowatch.com/2014/11/26/florida-ends-solar-incentive/
46   *Economist Laura D'Andrea Tyson wrote in June 2013:*
     http://economix.blogs.nytimes.com/2013/06/28/the-myriad-benefits-
     of-a-carbon-tax/?_r=0
52-62 *Earthship:*
     Earthship.com/systems.
     "Earthships include their own utilities made on site. An Earthship uses
     little to no fossil fuels to provide modern amenities. We are simply
     adapting our needs to the already existing activities of the planet."
53   Image Credit:
     http://earthship.com/Systems/
54   Illustration Credit:
     http://earthship.com/Designs/simple-survival.
     The Simple Survival Model Earthship provides its inhabitants with:
     1) comfortable shelter via very basic building techniques simplified
     from what has been learned on more-developed Earthship models,
     2) clean water via very basic water harvesting techniques,
     3) contained onsite sewage treatment while producing food and flora
     at the same time via very basic biological techniques, as well as
     4) an energy system that provides for the very basics of life via
     techniques.
55   Image Credit:
     http://earthship.com/Designs/global-model.
     All of the construction is designed to meet standard building code
     requirements.
56   Sample Interior Image Credit:
     http://www.rivendellvillage.org/huisvesting_eng.htm.
57   *Environmental activists and celebrities became interested...:*
     http://www.people.com/people/archive/article/0,,20114224,00.html.
57-62 *From Earthship.com:*
     http://earthship.com/codes-and-laws.

The site features 40 years of research and development of self-sufficient housing made from recycled materials.

5   Finance, Economics, and International Trade

64   *not enacted Section 956:*
        http://www.mondaq.com/unitedstates/x/283014/Financial+Services/
        Avoiding+the+Unintended+Tax+Consequences+of+Foreign+Subsidiary
        +Pledges+and+Guarantees+A+Look+at+Deemed+Dividends+in+US+Lo
        an+Transactions

64   *Wall Street bonuses in 2014 totaled $28,500,000,000 (for 167,800
        employees):* http://www.wsj.com/articles/wall-street-bonuses-grew-
        by-3-in-2014-to-28-5-billion-1426089740

64   *annual earnings of all full-time minimum wage workers:*
        http://www.motherjones.com/mojo/2015/03/income-inequality-
        chart-wall-street-bonuses-minimum-wage

65   https://www.philadelphiafed.org/publications/annual-
        report/2009/first-and-second-banks.cfm.

65   http://wiki.mises.org/wiki/Panic_of_1837

65   http://abrahamlincolnsclassroom.org/abraham-lincoln-in-
        depth/abraham-lincoln-banking-and-the-panic-of-1837-in-illinois/.

65   http://www.fas.harvard.edu/~histecon/crisis-
        next/1907/timeline.html#1907.

66   Europe and Central Banks, *New York Times*, January 9, 1910, Annual
        Financial Review, pg 8.

66   http://www.jekyllislandhistory.com/federalreserve.shtml

67   http://www.modernhistoryproject.org/mhp?Article=FedReserve&C=3.

67   https://www.law.cornell.edu/wex/taxing_power

67   http://www.federalreservehistory.org/Events/DetailView/18

67   *They made a deal*: https://www.jpmorgan.com/pages/company-
        history

68   *Federal Reserve contracts the money supply*:
        http://www.federalreservehistory.org/Events/DetailView/74

68   http://www.investopedia.com/terms/b/blackthursday.asp

68   http://www.pbs.org/wgbh/americanexperience/features/timeline/
        rails-timeline/.

68   https://news.google.com/newspapers?id=-
        q8fAAAAIBAJ&sjid=LdcEAAAAIBAJ&pg=2964,4612588&hl=en.

68   http://www.federalreservehistory.org/Events/DetailView/53.

68   http://www.newyorkfed.org/markets/statistics/dlyrates/fedrate.html.

69   http://www.nytimes.com/2008/10/03/business/03sec.html?page
      wanted=all.

70   http://www.washingtonpost.com/wp-
      dyn/content/article/2006/06/29/AR2006062900304.html.

71   http://www.forbes.com/sites/timworstall/2014/08/27/ben-bernanke-
      the-2008-financial-crisis-was-worse-than-the-great-depression/.

71   http://www.bloomberg.com/bw/stories/2008-09-26/jpmorgan-chase-
      to-buy-washington-mutualbusinessweek-business-news-stock-market-
      and-financial-advice.

71   http://www.moneycontrol.com/news-topic/jpmorgan-chase-bank/45.

72   http://www.cbpp.org/research/poverty-and-inequality/a-guide-to-
      statistics-on-historical-trends-in-income-inequality.

75   *"…a great vampire squid wrapped around the face of humanity,*
      relentlessly jamming its blood funnel into anything that smells like
      money." - Matt Taibbi, Rolling Stone investigative journalist describing
      Goldman Sachs http://www.rollingstone.com/politics/news/the-great-
      american-bubble-machine-20100405.

75   *This guy is so far up the financial industry's ass:*
      http://news.bbc.co.uk/2/hi/business/342086.stm.

76   *A PBS Frontline documentary, "The Warning,":*
      http://www.pbs.org/wgbh/pages/frontline/warning/.

76   *Rubin even contacted an old crony:*
      http://www.forbes.com/2002/02/11/0211rubin.html.

77   *In a 2009 Newsweek article:* http://www.newsweek.com/robert-
      rubin-how-make-capitalism-work-again-75809.

77   *Clinton called Rubin:*
      http://www.treasury.gov/about/history/pages/rerubin.aspx.

77   Clinton, Bill. *My Life*. New York: Knopf, 2004. Print.

79   *President Clinton slammed*: Ibid.

79   *The United States traded with the former Soviet Union during the Cold*
      War:
      http://fbnews.fb.org/FBNews/Special_Report/From_Cold_War_enem
      y_to_key_trade_partner--a_historical_look_at_U_S_-
      Russia_agricultural_trade.aspx.

79   *In 2000, Clinton said granting China Permanent Normal Trade*
      Relations:
      http://www.manufacturingnews.com/news/10/0615/WTO.html.

80   *83 billion dollars*:
      http://www.manufacturingnews.com/news/10/0615/WTO.html.

80   *273 billion dollars:*
      http://www.brookings.edu/research/opinions/2011/02/14-trade-

deficit-meltzer.

80 *General Motors now sells more cars in China than they do in the United States:* http://www.cnbc.com/id/100870316.

80 *G.M. even closed 13 plants after filing for bankruptcy but it opened 15 in China:* http://money.cnn.com/2011/01/20/news/international/us_business_chinese_investment_boom/.

81 *China operates on a complex policy depending upon economic mercantilism:* http://www.economist.com/blogs/freeexchange/2013/08/economic-history.

82 *China uses predatory pricing:* http://www.ft.com/intl/cms/s/0/42bd9a40-5900-11de-80b3-00144feabdc0.html#axzz3dAb7E2ng.

82 *it would rank as China's 8th largest trading partner:* http://www.huffingtonpost.com/al-norman/walmart-made-in-america_b_2523368.html.

82 *Rampant intellectual property theft by China is also rising:* http://thediplomat.com/2014/02/china-in-denial-about-addiction-to-ip-theft/.

83 *China's deliberately deceptive practices:* https://www.fas.org/sgp/crs/row/RS21625.pdf.

84 *the Chinese government slaps a 25% tax on it. However, when a consumer in the United States buys a Chinese product it is taxed at only 2.5%:* Ratigan, Dylan. *Greedy Bastards: How We Can Stop Corporate Communists, Banksters, and Other Vampires from Sucking America Dry.* New York: Simon & Schuster, 2012. Print.

85 http://www.bloomberg.com/slideshow/8/2012-03-30/inside-apple-s-foxconn-factory.html.

85 http://money.cnn.com/2015/01/27/technology/apple-iphone-earnings/.

85 *China is the largest holder of U.S. debt:* http://money.cnn.com/2015/05/18/news/economy/china-us-debt/.

86 http://www.investopedia.com/articles/forex/09/plaza-accord.asp.

87 http://www.japanfocus.org/-Dong-Wang/3958/article.html.

88 http://www.theatlantic.com/business/archive/2014/12/how-companies-hide-the-spoils-of-winning-government-contracts/383425/.

89 http://www.washingtonpost.com/opinions/harold-meyerson-money-made-at-others-expense/2014/01/28/61a275fc-8853-11e3-a5bd-844629433ba3_story.html.

90   http://www.businessinsider.com/dallas-fed-calls-for-breakup-of-big-banks-2012-3.

91   http://www.imf.org/external/pubs/ft/fandd/2015/03/jaumotte.htm.

92   *during the Eisenhower administration the top marginal tax rate (MTR) was 92 percent:* http://abcnews.go.com/Politics/eisenhower-obama-wealthy-americans-mitt-romney-pay-taxes/story?id=15387862#1.

92-93 http://robertreich.org/post/35591032374.

92   http://www.politifact.com/punditfact/statements/2014/jan/22/joe-scarborough/scarborough-top-1-took-95-gains-under-obama/.

94   http://www.forbes.com/sites/joelkotkin/2014/07/10/there-will-be-no-real-recovery-without-the-middle-class/.

6   Firearms

97   *Half of homeless veterans suffer from some form of mental illness and 70% have substance abuse problems*:
      http://nchv.org/index.php/news/media/background_and_statistics/

97   *Mentalhealth.gov reports:*
      http://www.mentalhealth.gov/basics/myths-facts/

97   *The Federal Substance Abuse and Mental Health Services Administration reports*: http://www.samhsa.gov/disorders

97   *Many states are dropping the ball:* http://familiesusa.org/product/50-state-look-medicaid-expansion

7   Immigration

101   *wake the Legislative Branch up*:
      http://www.uscis.gov/immigrationaction

102   *Federal reports show*: http://www.floridafarmbureau.org/node/2806

102   *Released a report*: Ibid.

102   *...are immigrants*: Ibid.

8   The Military vs. The Military-Industrial Complex

105   *cranks out surplus and then sells it to police departments, border patrols, and independent security organizations:*
      http://www.nytimes.com/2014/06/09/us/war-gear-flows-to-police-departments.html?_r=0

106   *"competing" for no-bid contracts:*
      http://www.publicintegrity.org/2011/08/29/5989/windfalls-war-pentagons-no-bid-contracts-triple-10-years-war

106   *push of a button in a control room*:
       http://nypost.com/2014/05/17/evolution-of-the-drone/

106   *with mass nuclear weapon use*: http://www.nti.org/threats/nuclear/

106   *additional aircraft carriers even the Pentagon says they don't need or want*:
       http://www.washingtontimes.com/news/2013/may/9/lawmakers-force-pentagon-to-buy-tanks-keep-ships-a/?page=all

107   http://www.eisenhower.archives.gov/research/online_documents/farewell_address.html.

9   Social Equality

111   *median hourly wage for women was 84% that of men during 2012 compared to 64% in 1980*:
       http://www.pewsocialtrends.org/2013/12/11/chapter-1-trends-from-government-data/.

111   *The division hardly moved in the past decade and the difference even expanded*: http://www.washingtonpost.com/opinions/five-myths-about-the-gender-pay-gap/2014/07/25/9e5cff34-fcd5-11e3-8176-f2c941cf35f1_story.html.

111   *Harvard economist, Claudia Godin says…*:
       http://www.nytimes.com/2014/04/24/upshot/the-pay-gap-is-because-of-gender-not-jobs.html?_r=2&abt=0002&abg=0.

111   *Gender discrimination accounts for 25 to 40 percent of the pay gap*:
       http://www.washingtonpost.com/opinions/five-myths-about-the-gender-pay-gap/2014/07/25/9e5cff34-fcd5-11e3-8176-f2c941cf35f1_story.html.

112   *Around 2/3 of U.S. children have both or their only parent working full-time*:
       https://www.americanprogress.org/issues/labor/news/2012/08/16/11978/fact-sheet-child-care/.

112   *Allowing more unionization has also been shown to narrow the difference*: http://www.uaw.org/articles/union-membership-narrows-earnings-gender-gap

112   *Raising the minimum wage will help women as 2/3 of workers making the minimum are female:* http://www.nwlc.org/our-issues/poverty-%2526-income-support/minimum-wage

112   *The World Economic Forum released a report*:
       http://www.weforum.org/news/2095-year-gender-equality-workplace-maybe

113   *Courts have decided that it is a violation of civil liberties to deny*

marriage based on race: https://www.aclu.org/loving-v-virginia-case-over-interracial-marriage.

116 *Supreme Court and Congress think that it's dead*: http://www.theguardian.com/commentisfree/2013/jun/25/supreme-court-voter-rights-act-racism-over

10   Social Security

119 *The Social Security program attempts to…:* http://ssa.gov/.

119 *average yearly benefit only $15,120*: http://www.fool.com/retirement/general/2015/01/17/the-average-american-gets-social-security-compare.aspx.

120 *Social Security has NOT contributed to federal deficit growth*: http://www.huffingtonpost.com/2012/12/12/social-security-fact-checkers-fiscal-cliff_n_2286462.html.

120 *Social Security is sustained by a dedicated payroll tax…:* http://www.ssa.gov/oact/progdata/taxRates.html.

120 *Ponzi scheme:* http://www.nytimes.com/2011/11/06/us/many-see-risk-in-rick-perrys-plan-for-social-security.html.

120 *He's (Rick Perry) grossly incorrect as usual:* http://www.nasdaq.com/article/why-social-security-is-not-a-ponzi-scheme-cm393166.

121 *The private sector controlling Social Security would be disastrous*: http://fortune.com/2010/11/30/privatizing-social-security-still-a-dumb-idea/.

122 *still be able to pay benefits at the current level until 2033 to 2037. At that point, EVEN WITHOUT MODIFICATION, revenues will be able to pay out 75% of promised benefits:* http://www.ssa.gov/oact/solvency/.

122 *solvent into the perceivable future:* http://www.cbsnews.com/news/is-social-security-broke-or-not/.

118 *Even at 1.9 workers per retiree in 2038, 81% of the current, inflation-adjusted rate would be paid out without increasing revenue at all:* http://mattbruenig.com/2011/08/16/the-myth-of-social-security-insolvency/.

11   Onward

125 *in his brilliant TED talk*: The TED site provides the following synopsis: "We can see the power of distributed, crowd-sourced business models

every day — witness Uber, Kickstarter, Airbnb. But veteran online activist Jeremy Heimans asks: When does that kind of 'new power' start to work in politics? His surprising answer: Sooner than you think. It's a bold argument about the future of politics and power; watch and see if you agree."
http://www.ted.com/talks/jeremy_heimans_what_new_power_looks _like?language=en.

131   Maher, Bill. *The New New Rules: A Funny Look at How Everybody But ME Has Their Head Up Their Ass*. New York: Plume, 2012. Print.

Sean Patrick Guthrie

ABOUT THE AUTHOR

Sean lives in Venice, Florida with his two dogs, Katniss and Vivian.

OTHER BOOKS BY SEAN PATRICK GUTHRIE

A comedic take on serious issues…

The Purple Dog Path to the U.S. Senate 2016 Official Companion Book: It Takes a Village idiot.

RECOMMENDED READING

A Fighting Chance
by Elizabeth Warren

Aftershock: The Next Economy and America's Future
by Robert B. Reich

Beyond Outrage: What Has Gone Wrong with Our Economy and Our Democracy, and How to Fix It
by Robert B. Reich

Greedy Bastards: How We Can Stop Corporate Communists, Banksters, and Other Vampires from Sucking America Dry
by Dylan Ratigan

ALSO AVAILABLE

The Purple Dog Path to the U.S. Senate 2016
Official Companion Book:
It Takes a Village idiot
by Sean Patrick Guthrie

Guthrie2016.com

Sean Patrick Guthrie